South

of

France

Jacques Casanova de Seingalt

[ZHINGOORA BOOKS]

This digital edition is published by Zhingoora Books.

The Cover is Designed by Pallav Sethiya.

SOUTH OF FRANCE

CHAPTER I

I Find Rosalie Happy—The Signora Isola-Bella—The Cook— Biribi—Irene—Possano in Prison—My Niece Proves to be an Old Friend of Rosalie's

At Genoa, where he was known to all, Pogomas called himself Possano. He introduced me to his wife and daughter, but they were so ugly and disgusting in every respect that I left them on some trifling pretext, and went to dine with my new niece. Afterwards I went to see the Marquis Grimaldi, for I longed to know what had become of Rosalie. The marquis was away in Venice, and was not expected back till the end of April; but one of his servants took me to Rosalie, who had become Madame Paretti six months after my departure.

My heart beat fast as I entered the abode of this woman, of whom I had such pleasant recollections. I first went to M. Paretti in his shop, and he received me with a joyful smile, which shewed me how happy he was. He took me to his wife directly, who cried out with delight, and ran to embrace me.

M. Paretti was busy, and begged me to excuse him, saying his wife would entertain me.

Rosalie shewed me a pretty little girl of six months old, telling me that she was happy, that she loved her husband, and was loved by him, that he was industrious and active in business, and under the patronage of the Marquis Grimaldi had prospered exceedingly.

The peaceful happiness of marriage had improved her wonderfully; she had become a perfect beauty in every sense of the word.

"My dear friend," she said, "you are very good to call on me directly you arrive, and I hope you will dine with us to-morrow. I owe all my happiness to you, and that is even a sweeter thought than the recollection of the passionate hours we have spent together. Let us kiss, but no more; my duty as an honest wife forbids me from going any further, so do not disturb the happiness you have given."

I pressed her hand tenderly, to skew that I assented to the conditions she laid down.

"Oh! by the way," she suddenly exclaimed, "I have a pleasant surprise for you."

She went out, and a moment afterward returned with Veronique, who had become her maid. I was glad to see her and embraced her affectionately, asking after Annette. She said her sister was well, and was working with her mother.

"I want her to come and wait on my niece while we are here," said I.

At this Rosalie burst out laughing.

"What! another niece? You have a great many relations! But as she is your niece, I hope you will bring her with you to-morrow."

"Certainly, and all the more willingly as she is from Marseilles."

"From Marseilles? Why, we might know each other. Not that that would matter, for all your nieces are discreet young persons. What is her name?"

"Crosin."

"I don't know it."

"I daresay you don't. She is the daughter of a cousin of mine who lived at Marseilles."

"Tell that to someone else; but, after all, what does it matter? You choose well, amuse yourself, and make them happy. It may be wisdom after all, and at any rate I congratulate you. I shall be delighted to see your niece, but if she knows me you must see that she knows her part as well."

On leaving Madame Paretti I called on the Signora Isola-Bella, and gave her the Marquis Triulzi's letter. Soon after she came into the room and welcomed me, saying that she had been expecting me, as Triulzi had written to her on the subject. She introduced me to the Marquis Augustino Grimaldi delta Pietra, her 'cicisbeoin-chief' during the long absence of her husband, who lived at Lisbon.

The signora's apartments were very elegant. She was pretty with small though regular features, her manner was pleasant, her voice sweet, and her figure well shaped, though too thin. She was nearly thirty. I say nothing of her complexion, for her face was plastered with white and red, and so coarsely, that these patches of paint were the first things that caught my attention. I was disgusted at this, in spite of her fine expressive eyes. After an hour spent in question and reply, in which both parties were feeling their way, I accepted her invitation to come to supper on the following day. When I got back I complimented my niece on the way in which she had arranged her room, which was only separated from mine by a small closet which I intended for her maid, who, I told her, was coming the next day. She was highly pleased with this attention, and it paved the way for my success. I also told her that the next day she was to dine with me at a substantial merchant's as my niece, and this piece of news made her quite happy.

This girl whom Croce had infatuated and deprived of her senses was exquisitely beautiful, but more charming than all her physical beauties were the nobleness of her presence and the sweetness of her disposition. I was already madly in love with her, and I repented not having taken possession of her on the first day of our journey. If I had taken her at her word I should have been a steadfast lover, and I do not think it would have taken me long to make her forget her former admirer.

I had made but a small dinner, so I sat down to supper famishing with hunger; and as my niece had an excellent appetite we prepared ourselves for enjoyment, but instead of the dishes being delicate, as we had expected, they were detestable. I told Clairmont to send for the landlady, and she said that she could not help it, as everything had been done by my own cook.

"My cook?" I repeated.

"Yes, sir, the one your secretary, M. Possano, engaged for you. I could have got a much better one and a much cheaper one myself."

"Get one to-morrow."

"Certainly; but you must rid yourself and me of the present cook, for he has taken up his position here with his wife and children. Tell Possano to send for him."

"I will do so, and in the meanwhile do you get me a fresh cook. I will try him the day after to-morrow."

I escorted my niece into her room, and begged her to go to bed without troubling about me, and so saying I took up the paper and began to read it. When I had finished, I went up to bed, and said,

"You might spare me the pain of having to sleep by myself."

She lowered her eyes but said nothing, so I gave her a kiss and left her.

In the morning my fair niece came into my room just as Clairmont was washing my feet, and begged me to let her have some coffee as chocolate made her hot. I told my man to go and fetch some coffee, and as soon as he was gone she went down on her knees and would have wiped my feet.

"I cannot allow that, my dear young lady."

"Why not? it is a mark of friendship."

"That may be, but such marks cannot be given to anyone but your lover without your degrading yourself."

She got up and sat down on a chair quietly, but saying nothing.

Clairmont came back again, and I proceeded with my toilette.

The landlady came in with our breakfast, and asked my niece if she would like to buy a fine silk shawl made in the Genoese fashion. I did not let her be confused by having to answer, but told the landlady to let us see it. Soon after the milliner came in, but by that time I had given my young friend twenty Genoese sequins, telling her that she might use them for her private wants. She took the money, thanking me with much grace, and letting me imprint a delicious kiss on her lovely lips.

I had sent away the milliner after having bought the shawl, when Possano took it upon himself to remonstrate with me in the matter of the cook.

"I engaged the man by your orders," said he, "for the whole time you stayed at Genoa, at four francs a day, with board and lodging."

"Where is my letter?"

"Here it is: 'Get me a good cook; I will keep him while I stay in Genoa.'"

"Perhaps you did not remark the expression, a good cook? Well, this fellow is a very bad cook; and, at all events, I am the best judge whether he is good or bad."

"You are wrong, for the man will prove his skill. He will cite you in the law courts, and win his case."

"Then you have made a formal agreement with him?"

"Certainly; and your letter authorized me to do so."

"Tell him to come up; I want to speak to him."

While Possano was downstairs I told Clairmont to go and fetch me an advocate. The cook came upstairs, I read the agreement, and I saw that it was worded in such a manner that I should be in the wrong legally; but I did not change my mind for all that.

"Sir," said the cook, "I am skilled in my business, and I can get four thousand Genoese to swear as much."

"That doesn't say much for their good taste; but whatever they may-say, the execrable supper you gave me last night proves that you are only fit to keep a low eating-house."

As there is nothing more irritable than the feelings of a culinary artist, I was expecting a sharp answer; but just then the advocate came in. He had heard the end of our dialogue, and told me that not only would the man find plenty of witnesses to his skill, but that I should find a very great difficulty in getting anybody at all to swear to his want of skill.

"That may be," I replied, "but as I stick to my own opinion, and think his cooking horrible, he must go, for I want to get another, and I will pay that fellow as if he had served me the whole time."

"That won't do," said the cook; "I will summon you before the judge and demand damages for defamation of character."

At this my bile overpowered me, and I was going to seize him and throw him out of the window, when Don Antonio Grimaldi came in. When he heard what was the matter, he laughed and said, with a shrug of his shoulders,

"My dear sir, you had better not go into court, or you will be cast in costs, for the evidence is against you. Probably this man makes a slight mistake in believing himself to be an excellent cook, but the chief mistake is in the agreement, which ought to have stipulated that he should cook a trial dinner. The person who drew up the agreement is either a great knave or a great fool."

At this Possano struck in in his rude way, and told the nobleman that he was neither knave nor fool.

"But you are cousin to the cook," said the landlady.

This timely remark solved the mystery. I paid and dismissed the advocate, and having sent the cook out of the room I said,

"Do I owe you any money, Possano?"

"On the contrary, you paid me a month in advance, and there are ten more days of the month to run."

"I will make you a present of the ten days and send you away this very moment, unless your cousin does not leave my house to-day, and give you the foolish engagement which you signed in my name."

"That's what I call cutting the Gordian knot," said M. Grimaldi.

He then begged me to introduce him to the lady he had seen with me, and I did so, telling him she was my niece.

"Signora Isola-Bella will be delighted to see her."

"As the marquis did not mention her in his letter, I did not take the liberty of bringing her."

The marquis left a few moments afterwards, and soon after Annette came in with her mother. The girl had developed in an incredible manner while I was away. Her cheeks blossomed like the rose, her teeth were white as pearls, and her breasts, though modestly concealed from view, were exquisitely rounded. I presented her to her mistress, whose astonishment amused me.

Annette, who looked pleased to be in my service again, went to dress her new mistress; and, after giving a few sequins to the mother I sent her away, and proceeded to make my toilette.

Towards noon, just as I was going out with my niece to dine at Rosalie's, my landlady brought me the agreement Possano had made, and introduced the new cook. I ordered the next day's dinner, and went away much pleased with my comic victory.

A brilliant company awaited us at the Paretti's, but I was agreeably surprised on introducing my niece to Rosalie to see them recognize each other. They called each other by their respective names, and indulged in an affectionate embrace. After this they retired to another room for a quarter of an hour, and returned looking very happy. Just then Paretti entered, and on Rosalie introducing him to my niece under her true name he welcomed her in the most cordial manner. Her father was a correspondent of his, and drawing a letter he had just received from him from his pocket, he gave it to her to read. My niece read it eagerly, with tears in her eyes, and gave the signature a respectful pressure with her lips. This expression of filial love, which displayed all the feelings of her heart, moved me to such an extent that I burst into tears. Then taking Rosalie aside, I begged her to ask her husband not to mention the fact to his correspondent that he had seen his daughter.

The dinner was excellent, and Rosalie did the honours with that grace which was natural to her. However, the guests did not by any means pay her all their attentions, the greater portion of which was diverted in the direction of my supposed niece. Her father, a prosperous merchant of Marseilles, was well known in the commercial circles of Genoa, and besides this her wit and beauty captivated everybody, and one young gentleman fell madly in love with her. He was an extremely good match, and proved to be the husband whom Heaven had destined for my charming friend. What a happy thought it was for me that I had been the means of rescuing her from the gulf of shame, misery, and despair, and placing her on the high road to happiness. I own that I have always felt a keener pleasure in doing good than in anything else, though, perhaps, I may not always have done good from strictly disinterested motives.

When we rose from the table in excellent humour with ourselves and our surroundings, cards were proposed, and Rosalie, who knew my likings, said it must be trente-quarante. This was agreed to, and we played till supper, nobody either winning or losing to any extent. We did not go till midnight, after having spent a very happy day.

When we were in our room I asked my niece how she had known Rosalie.

"I knew her at home; she and her mother used to bring linen from the wash. I always liked her."

"You must be nearly the same age."

"She is two years older than I am. I recognized her directly."

"What did she tell you?"

"That it was you who brought her from Marseilles and made her fortune."

"She has not made you the depositary of any other confidences?"

"No, but there are some things which don't need telling."

"You are right. And what did you tell her?"

"Only what she could have guessed for herself. I told her that you were not my uncle, and if she thought you were my lover I was not sorry. You do not know how I have enjoyed myself to-day, you must have been born to make me happy."

"But how about La Croix?"

"For heaven's sake say nothing about him."

This conversation increased my ardour. She called Annette, and I went to my room.

As I had expected, Annette came to me as soon as her mistress was in bed.

"If the lady is really your niece," said she, "may I hope that you still love me?"

"Assuredly, dear Annette, I shall always love you. Undress, and let us have a little talk."

I had not long to wait, and in the course of two voluptuous hours I quenched the flames that another woman had kindled in my breast.

Next morning Possano came to tell me that he had arranged matters with the cook with the help of six sequins. I gave him the money, and told him to be more careful for the future.

I went to Rosalie's for my breakfast, which she was delighted to give me: and I asked her and her husband to dinner on the following day, telling her to bring any four persons she liked.

"Your decision," said I, "will decide the fate of my cook; it will be his trial dinner."

She promised to come, and then pressed me to tell her the history of my amours with her fair country-woman.

"Alas!" I said, "you may not believe me, but I assure you I am only beginning with her."

"I shall certainly believe you, if you tell me so, though it seems very strange."

"Strange but true. You must understand, however, that I have only known her for a very short time; and, again, I would not be made happy save through love, mere submission would kill me."

"Good! but what did she say of me?"

I gave her a report of the whole conversation I had had with my niece the night before, and she was delighted."

"As you have not yet gone far with your niece, would you object if the young man who shewed her so much attention yesterday were of the party to-morrow?"

"Who is he? I should like to know him."

"M. N——, the only son of a rich merchant."

"Certainly, bring him with you."

When I got home I went to my niece, who was still in bed, and told her that her fellow-countryman would dine with us to-morrow. I comforted her with the assurance that M. Paretti would not tell her father that she was in Genoa. She had been a good deal tormented with the idea that the merchant would inform her father of all.

As I was going out to supper I told her that she could go and sup with
Rosalie, or take supper at home if she preferred it.

"You are too kind to me, my dear uncle. I will go to Rosalie's."

"Very good. Are you satisfied with Annette?"

"Oh! by the way, she told me that you spent last night with her, and that you had been her lover and her sister's at the same time."

"It is true, but she is very indiscreet to say anything about it."

"We must forgive her, though. She told me that she only consented to sleep with you on the assurance that I was really your niece. I am sure she only made this confession out of vanity, and in the hope of gaining my favour, which would be naturally bestowed on a woman you love."

"I wish you had the right to be jealous of her; and I swear that if she does not comport herself with the utmost obedience to you in every respect, I will send her packing, in despite of our relations. As for you, you may not be able to love me, and I have no right to complain; but I will not have you degrade yourself by becoming my submissive victim."

I was not sorry for my niece to know that I made use of Annette, but my vanity was wounded at the way she took it. It was plain that she was not at all in love with me, and that she was glad that there was a safeguard in the person of her maid, and that thus we could be together without danger, for she could not ignore the power of her charms.

We dined together, and augured well of the skill of the new cook. M. Paretti had promised to get me a good man, and he presented himself just as we were finishing dinner, and I made a present of him to my niece. We went for a drive together, and I left my niece at Rosalie's, and I then repaired to Isola-Bella's, where I found a numerous and brilliant company had assembled consisting of all the best people in Genoa.

Just then all the great ladies were mad over 'biribi', a regular cheating game. It was strictly forbidden at Genoa, but this only made it more popular, and besides, the prohibition had no force in private houses, which are outside of the jurisdiction of the Government; in short, I found the game in full swing at the Signora Isola-Bella's. The professional gamesters who kept the bank went from house to house, and the amateurs were advised of their presence at such a house and at such a time.

Although I detested the game, I began to play—to do as the others did.

In the room there was a portrait of the mistress of the house in harlequin costume, and there happened to be the same picture on one of the divisions of the biribi-table: I chose this one out of politeness, and did not play on any other. I risked a sequin each time. The board had thirty-six compartments, and if one lost, one paid thirty-two times the amount of the stake; this, of course, was an enormous advantage for the bank.

Each player drew three numbers in succession, and there were three professionals; one kept the bag, another the bank, and the third the board, and the last took care to gather in the winnings as soon as the result was known, and the bank amounted to two thousand sequins or thereabouts. The table, the cloth, and four silver candlesticks belonged to the players.

I sat at the left of Madame Isola-Bella, who began to play, and as there were fifteen or sixteen of us I had lost about fifty sequins when my turn came, for my harlequin had not appeared once. Everybody pitied me, or pretended to do so, for selfishness is the predominant passion of gamesters.

My turn came at last. I drew my harlequin and received thirty-two sequins. I left them on the same figure, and got a thousand sequins. I left fifty still on the board, and the harlequin came out for the third time. The bank was broken, and the table, the cloth, the candlesticks, and the board all belonged to me. Everyone congratulated me, and the wretched bankrupt gamesters were hissed, hooted, and turned out of doors.

After the first transports were over, I saw that the ladies were in distress; for as there could be no more gaming they did not know what to do. I consoled them by declaring that I would be banker, but with equal stakes, and that I would pay winning cards thirty-six times the stake instead of thirty-two. This was pronounced charming of me, and I amused everybody till supper-time, without any great losses or gains on either side. By dint of entreaty I made the lady of the house accept the whole concern as a present, and a very handsome one it was.

The supper was pleasant enough, and my success at play was the chief topic of conversation. Before leaving I asked Signora Isola-Bella and her marquis to dine with me, and they eagerly accepted the invitation. When I got home I went to see my niece, who told me she had spent a delightful evening.

"A very pleasant young man," said she, "who is coming to dine with us to-morrow, paid me great attention."

"The same, I suppose, that did so yesterday?"

"Yes. Amongst other pretty things he told me that if I liked he would go to Marseilles and ask my hand of my father. I said nothing, but I thought to myself that if the poor young man gave himself all this trouble he would be woefully misled, as he would not see me."

"Why not?"

"Because I should be in a nunnery. My kind good father will forgive me, but I must punish myself."

"That is a sad design, which I hope you will abandon. You have all that would make the happiness of a worthy husband. The more I think it over, the more I am convinced of the truth of what I say."

We said no more just then, for she needed rest. Annette came to undress her, and I was glad to see the goodness of my niece towards her, but the coolness with which the girl behaved to her mistress did not escape my notice. As soon as she came to sleep with me I gently remonstrated with her, bidding her to do her duty better for the future. Instead of answering with a caress, as she ought to have done, she began to cry.

"My dear child," said I, "your tears weary me. You are only here to amuse me, and if you can't do that, you had better go."

This hurt her foolish feelings of vanity, and she got up and went away without a word, leaving me to go to sleep in a very bad temper.

In the morning I told her, in a stern voice, that if she played me such a trick again I would send her away. Instead of trying to soothe me with a kiss the little rebel burst out crying again. I sent her out of the room impatiently, and proceeded to count my gains.

I thought no more about it, but presently my niece came in and asked me why I had vexed poor Annette.

"My dear niece," said I, "tell her to behave better or else I will send her back to her mother's."

She gave me no reply, but took a handful of silver and fled. I had not time to reflect on this singular conduct, for Annette came in rattling her crowns in her pocket, and promised, with a kiss, not to make me angry any more.

Such was my niece. She knew I adored her, and she loved me; but she did not want me to be her lover, though she made use of the ascendancy which my passion gave her. In the code of feminine coquetry such cases are numerous.

Possano came uninvited to see me, and congratulated me on my victory of the evening before.

"Who told you about it?"

"I have just been at the coffee-house, where everybody is talking of it. It was a wonderful victory, for those biribanti are knaves of the first water. Your adventure is making a great noise, for everyone says that you could not have broken their bank unless you had made an agreement with the man that kept the bag."

"My dear fellow, I am tired of you. Here, take this piece of money for your wife and be off."

The piece of money I had given him was a gold coin worth a hundred Genoese livres, which the Government had struck for internal commerce; there were also pieces of fifty and twenty-five livres.

I was going on with my calculations when Clairmont brought me a note. It was from Irene, and contained a tender invitation to breakfast with her. I did not know that she was in Genoa, and the news gave me very great pleasure. I locked up my money, dressed in haste, and started out to see her. I found her in good and well-furnished rooms, and her old father, Count Rinaldi, embraced me with tears of joy.

After the ordinary compliments had been passed, the old man proceeded to congratulate me on my winnings of the night before.

"Three thousand sequins!" he exclaimed, "that is a grand haul indeed."

"Quite so."

"The funny part of it is that the man who keeps the bag is in the pay of the others."

"What strikes you as funny in that?"

"Why, he gained half without any risk, otherwise he would not have been likely to have entered into an agreement with you."

"You think, then, that it was a case of connivance?"

"Everybody says so; indeed what else could it be? The rascal has made his fortune without running any risk. All the Greeks in Genoa are applauding him and you."

"As the greater rascal of the two?"

"They don't call you a rascal; they say you're a great genius; you are praised and envied."

"I am sure I ought to be obliged to them."

"I heard it all from a gentleman who was there. He says that the second and the third time the man with the bag gave you the office."

"And you believe this?"

"I am sure of it. No man of honour in your position could have acted otherwise. However, when you come to settle up with the fellow I advise you to be very careful, for there will be spies on your tracks. If you like, I will do the business for you."

I had enough self-restraint to repress the indignation and rage I felt. Without a word I took my hat and marched out of the room, sternly repulsing Irene who tried to prevent me from going as she had done once before. I resolved not to have anything more to do with the wretched old count.

This calumnious report vexed me extremely, although I knew that most gamesters would consider it an honour. Possano and Rinaldi had said enough to shew me that all the town was talking over it, and I was not surprised that everyone believed it; but for my part I did not care to be taken for a rogue when I had acted honourably.

I felt the need of unbosoming myself to someone, and walked towards the Strada Balbi to call on the Marquis Grimaldi, and discuss the matter with him. I was told he was gone to the courts, so I followed him there and was ushered into vast hall, where he waited on me. I told him my story, and he said,

"My dear chevalier, you ought to laugh at it, and I should not advise you to take the trouble to refute the calumny."

"Then you advise me to confess openly that I am a rogue?"

"No, for only fools will think that of you. Despise them, unless they tell you you are a rogue to your face."

"I should like to know the name of the nobleman who was present and sent this report about the town."

"I do not know who it is. He was wrong to say anything, but you would be equally wrong in taking any steps against him, for I am sure he did not tell the story with any intention of giving offence; quite the contrary."

"I am lost in wonder at his course of reasoning. Let us suppose that the facts were as he told them, do you think they are to my honour?"

"Neither to your honour nor shame. Such are the morals and such the maxims of gamesters. The story will be laughed at, your skill will be applauded, and you will be admired, for each one will say that in your place he would have done likewise!"

"Would you?"

"Certainly. If I had been sure that the ball would have gone to the harlequin, I would have broken the rascal's bank, as you did. I will say honestly that I do not know whether you won by luck or skill, but the most probable hypothesis, to my mind, is that you knew the direction of the ball. You must confess that there is something to be said in favour of the supposition."

"I confess that there is, but it is none the less a dishonourable imputation on me, and you in your turn must confess that those who think that I won by sleight of hand, or by an agreement with a rascal, insult me grievously."

"That depends on the way you look at it. I confess they insult you, if you think yourself insulted; but they are not aware of that, and their intention being quite different there is no insult at all in the matter. I promise you no one will tell you to your face that you cheated, but how are you going to prevent them thinking so?"

"Well, let them think what they like, but let them take care not to tell me their thoughts."

I went home angry with Grimaldi, Rinaldi, and everyone else. My anger vexed me, I should properly have only laughed, for in the state of morals at Genoa, the accusation, whether true or false, could not injure my honour. On the contrary I gained by it a reputation for being a genius, a term which the Genoese prefer to that Methodistical word, "a rogue," though the meaning is the same. Finally I was astonished to find myself reflecting that I should have had no scruple in breaking the bank in the way suggested, if it had only been for the sake of making the company laugh. What vexed me most was that I was credited with an exploit I had not performed.

When dinner-time drew near I endeavoured to overcome my ill temper for the sake of the company I was going to receive. My niece was adorned only with her native charms, for the rascal Croce had sold all her jewels; but she was elegantly dressed, and her beautiful hair was more precious than a crown of rubies.

Rosalie came in richly dressed and looking very lovely. Her husband, her uncle, and her aunt were with her, and also two friends, one of whom was the aspirant for the hand of my niece.

Madame Isola-Bella and her shadow, M. Grimaldi, came late, like great people. Just as we were going to sit down, Clairmont told me that a man wanted to speak to me.

"Shew him in."

As soon as he appeared M. Grimaldi exclaimed:

"The man with the bag!"

"What do you want?" I said, dryly.

"Sir, I am come to ask you to help me. I am a family man, and it is thought that . . ."

I did not let him finish.

"I have never refused to aid the unfortunate," said I. "Clairmont, give him ten sequins. Leave the room."

This incident spoke in my favour, and made me in a better temper.

We sat down to table, and a letter was handed to me. I recognized Possano's writing, and put it in my pocket without reading it.

The dinner was delicious, and my cook was pronounced to have won his spurs. Though her exalted rank and the brilliance of her attire gave Signora Isoía-Bella the first place of right, she was nevertheless eclipsed by my two nieces. The young Genoese was all attention for the fair Marseillaise, and I could see that she was not displeased. I sincerely wished to see her in love with someone, and I liked her too well to bear the idea of her burying herself in a convent. She could never be happy till she found someone who would make her forget the rascal who had brought her to the brink of ruin.

I seized the opportunity, when all my guests were engaged with each other, to open Possano's letter. It ran as follows:

"I went to the bank to change the piece of gold you gave me. It was weighed, and found to be ten carats under weight. I was told to name the person from whom I got it, but of course I did not do so. I then had to go to prison, and if you do not get me out of the scrape

I shall be prosecuted, though of course I am not going to get myself hanged for anybody."

I gave the letter to Grimaldi, and when we had left the table he took me aside, and said,—

"This is a very serious matter, for it may end in the gallows for the man who clipped the coin."

"Then they can hang the biribanti! That won't hurt me much."

"No, that won't do; it would compromise Madame Isola-Bella, as biribi is strictly forbidden. Leave it all to me, I will speak to the State Inquisitors about it. Tell Possano to persevere in his silence, and that you will see him safely through. The laws against coiners and clippers are only severe with regard to these particular coins, as the Government has special reasons for not wishing them to be depreciated."

I wrote to Possano, and sent for a pair of scales. We weighed the gold I had won at biribi, and every single piece had been clipped. M. Grimaldi said he would have them defaced and sold to a jeweller.

When we got back to the dining-room we found everybody at play. M. Grimaldi proposed that I should play at quinze with him. I detested the game, but as he was my guest I felt it would be impolite to refuse, and in four hours I had lost five hundred sequins.

Next morning the marquis told me that Possano was out of prison, and that he had been given the value of the coin. He brought me thirteen hundred sequins which had resulted from the sale of the gold. We agreed that I was to call on Madame Isola-Bella the next day, when he would give me my revenge at quinze.

I kept the appointment, and lost three thousand sequins. I paid him a thousand the next day, and gave him two bills of exchange, payable by myself, for the other two thousand. When these bills were presented I was in England, and being badly off I had to have them protested. Five years later, when I was at Barcelona, M. de Grimaldi was urged by a traitor to have me imprisoned, but he knew enough of me to be sure that if I did not meet the bills it was from sheer inability to do so. He even wrote me a very polite letter, in which he gave the name of my enemy, assuring me that he would never take any steps to compel me to pay the money. This enemy was Possano, who was also at Barcelona, though I was not aware of his presence. I will speak of the circumstance in due time, but I cannot help remarking that all who aided me in my pranks with Madame d'Urfe proved traitors, with the exception of a Venetian girl, whose acquaintance the reader will make in the following chapter.

In spite of my losses I enjoyed myself, and had plenty of money, for after all I had only lost what I had won at biribi. Rosalie often dined with us, either alone or with her husband, and I supped regularly at her home with my niece, whose love affair seemed quite promising. I congratulated her upon the circumstance, but she persisted in her determination to take refuge from the world in a cloister. Women often do the most idiotic things out of sheer obstinacy; possibly they deceive even themselves, and act in good faith; but unfortunately, when the veil falls from before their eyes, they see but the profound abyss into which their folly had plunged them.

In the meanwhile, my niece had become so friendly and familiar that she would often come and sit on my bed in the morning when Annette was still in my arms. Her presence increased my ardour, and I quenched the fires on the blonde which the brunette was kindling. My niece seemed to enjoy the sight, and I could see that her senses were being pleasantly tortured. Annette was short-sighted, and so did not perceive my distractions, while my fair niece caressed me slightly, knowing that it would add to my pleasures. When she thought I was exhausted she told Annette to get up and leave me alone with her, as she wanted to tell me something. She then began to jest and toy, and though her dress was extremely disordered she seemed to think that her charms would exercise no power over me. She was quite mistaken, but I was careful not to undeceive her for fear of losing her confidence. I watched the game carefully, and noting how little by little her familiarity increased, I felt sure that she would have to surrender at last, if not at Genoa, certainly on the journey, when we would be thrown constantly in each other's society with nobody to spy upon our actions, and with nothing else to do but to make love. It is the weariness of a journey, the constant monotony, that makes one do something to make sure of one's existence; and when it comes to the reckoning there is usually more joy than repentance.

But the story of my journey from Genoa to Marseilles was written in the book of fate, and could not be read by me. All I knew was that I must soon go as Madame d'Urfe was waiting for me at Marseilles. I knew not that in this journey would be involved the fate of a Venetian girl of whom I had never heard, who had never seen me, but whom I was destined to render happy. My fate seemed to have made me stop at Genoa to wait for her.

I settled my accounts with the banker, to whom I had been accredited, and I took a letter of credit on Marseilles, where, however, I was not likely to want for funds, as my high treasurer, Madame d'Urfe was there. I took leave of Madame Isola-Bella and her circle that I might be able to devote all my time to Rosalie and her friends.

CHAPTER II

Disgraceful Behaviour of My Brother, the Abbe, I Relieve Him of His Mistress—Departure from Genoa—The Prince of Monaco—My Niece Overcome—Our Arrival at Antibes

On the Tuesday in Holy Week I was just getting up, when Clairmont came to tell me that a priest who would not give his name wanted to speak to me. I went out in my night-cap, and the rascally priest rushed at me and nearly choked me with his embraces. I did not like so much affection, and as I had not recognized him at first on account of the darkness of the room, I took him by the arm and led him to the window. It was my youngest brother, a good-for-nothing fellow, whom I had always disliked. I had not seen him for ten years, but I cared so little about him that I had not even enquired whether he were alive or dead in the correspondence I maintained with M. de Bragadin, Dandolo, and Barbaro.

As soon as his silly embraces were over, I coldly asked him what chance had brought him to Genoa in this disgusting state of dirt, rags, and tatters. He was only twenty-nine, his complexion was fresh and healthy, and he had a splendid head of hair. He was a posthumous son, born like Mahomet, three months after the death of his father.

"The story of my misfortunes would be only too long. Take me into your room, and I will sit down and tell you the whole story."

"First of all, answer my questions. How long have you been here?"

"Since yesterday."

"Who told you that I was here?"

"Count B——, at Milan."

"Who told you that the count knew me?"

"I found out by chance. I was at M. de Bragadin's a month ago, and on his table I saw a letter from the count to you."

"Did you tell him you were my brother?"

"I had to when he said how much I resembled you."

"He made a mistake, for you are a blockhead."

"He did not think so, at all events, for he asked me to dinner."

"You must have cut a pretty figure, if you were in your present state."

"He gave me four sequins to come here; otherwise, I should never have been able to do the journey."

"Then he did a very foolish thing. You're a mere beggar, then; you take alms. Why did you leave Venice? What do you want with me? I can do nothing for you."

"Ah! do not make me despair, or I shall kill myself."

"That's the very best thing you could do; but you are too great a coward. I ask again why you left Venice, where you could say mass, and preach, and make an honest living, like many priests much better than you?"

"That is the kernel of the whole matter. Let us go in and I will tell you."

"No; wait for me here. We will go somewhere where you can tell me your story, if I have patience to listen to it. But don't tell any of my people that you are my brother, for I am ashamed to have such a relation. Come, take me to the place where you are staying."

"I must tell you that at my inn I am not alone, and I want to have a private interview with you."

"Who is with you?"

"I will tell you presently, but let us go into a coffeehouse."

"Are you in company with a band of brigands? What are you sighing at?"

"I must confess it, however painful it may be to my feelings. I am with a woman."

"A woman! and you a priest!"

"Forgive me. I was blinded by love, and seduced by my senses and her beauty, so I seduced her under a promise to marry her at Geneva. I can never go back to Venice, for I took her away from her father's house."

"What could you do at Geneva? They would expel you after you had been there three or four days. Come, we will go to the inn and see the woman you have deceived. I will speak to you afterwards."

I began to trace my steps in the direction he had pointed out, and he was obliged to follow me. As soon as we got to the inn, he went on in front, and after climbing three flights of stairs I entered a wretched den where I saw a tall young girl, a sweet brunette, who looked proud and not in the least confused. As soon as I made my appearance she said, without any greeting,—

"Are you the brother of this liar and monster who has deceived me so abominably?"

"Yes," said I. "I have the honour."

"A fine honour, truly. Well, have the kindness to send me back to Venice, for I won't stop any longer with this rascal whom I listened to like the fool I was, who turned my head with his lying tales. He was going to meet you at Milan, and you were to give us enough money to go to Geneva, and there we were to turn Protestants and get married. He swore you were expecting him at Milan, but you were not there at all, and he contrived to get money in some way or another, and brought me here miserably enough. I thank Heaven he has found you at last, for if he had not I should have started off by myself and begged my way. I have not a single thing left; the wretch sold all I possessed at Bergamo and Verona. I don't know how I kept my senses through it all. To hear him talk, the world was a paradise outside Venice, but I have found to my cost that there is no place like home. I curse the hour when I first saw the miserable wretch. He's a beggarly knave; always whining. He wanted to enjoy his rights as my husband when we got to Padua, but I am thankful to say I gave him nothing. Here is the writing he gave me; take it, and do what you like with it. But if you have any heart, send me back to Venice or I will tramp there on foot."

I had listened to this long tirade without interrupting her. She might have spoken at much greater length, so far as I was concerned; my astonishment took my breath away. Her discourse had all the fire of eloquence, and was heightened by her expressive face and the flaming glances she shot from her eyes.

My brother, sitting down with his head between his hands, and obliged to listen in silence to this long catalogue of well-deserved reproaches, gave something of a comic element to the scene. In spite of that, however, I was much touched by the sad aspects of the girl's story. I felt at once that I must take charge of her, and put an end to this ill-assorted match. I imagined that I should not have much difficulty in sending her back to Venice, which she might never have quitted if it had not been for her trust in me, founded on the fallacious promises of her seducer.

The true Venetian character of the girl struck me even more than her beauty. Her courage, frank indignation, and the nobility of her aspect made me resolve not to abandon her. I could not doubt that she had told a true tale, as my brother continued to observe a guilty silence.

I watched her silently for some time, and, my mind being made up, said,—

"I promise to send you back to Venice with a respectable woman to look after you; but you will be unfortunate if you carry back with you the results of your amours."

"What results? Did I not tell you that we were going to be married at
Geneva?"

"Yes, but in spite of that . . ."

"I understand you, sir, but I am quite at ease on that point, as I am happy to say that I did not yield to any of the wretch's desires."

"Remember," said the abbe, in a plaintive voice, "the oath you took to be mine for ever. You swore it upon the crucifix."

So saying he got up and approached her with a supplicating gesture, but as soon as he was within reach she gave him a good hearty box on the ear. I expected to see a fight, in which I should not have interfered, but nothing of the kind. The humble abbe gently turned away to the window, and casting his eyes to heaven began to weep.

"You are too malicious, my dear," I said; "the poor devil is only unhappy because you have made him in love with you."

"If he is it's his own fault, I should never have thought of him but for his coming to me and fooling me, I shall never forgive him till he is out of my sight. That's not the first blow I have given him; I had to begin at Padua."

"Yes," said the abbe, "but you are excommunicated, for I am a priest."

"It's little I care for the excommunication of a scoundrel like you, and if you say another word I will give you some more."

"Calm yourself, my child," said I; "you have cause to be angry, but you should not beat him. Take up your things and follow me."

"Where are you going to take her?" said the foolish priest.

"To my own house, and I should advise you to hold your tongue. Here, take these twenty sequins and buy yourself some clean clothes and linen, and give those rags of yours to the beggars. I will come and talk to you to-morrow, and you may thank your stars that you found me here. As for you, mademoiselle, I will have you conducted to my lodging, for Genoa must not see you in my company after arriving here with a priest. We must not have any scandal. I shall place you under the charge of my landlady, but whatever you do don't tell her this sad story. I will see that you are properly dressed, and that you want for nothing."

"May Heaven reward you!"

My brother, astonished at the sight of the twenty sequins, let me go away without a word. I had the fair Venetian taken to my lodging in a sedan-chair, and putting her under the charge of my landlady I told the latter to see that she was properly dressed. I wanted to see how she would look in decent clothes, for her present rags and tatters detracted from her appearance. I warned Annette that a girl who had been placed in my care would eat and sleep with her, and then having to entertain a numerous company of guests I proceeded to make my toilette.

Although my niece had no rights over me, I valued her esteem, and thought it best to tell her the whole story lest she should pass an unfavourable judgment on me. She listened attentively and thanked me for my confidence in her, and said she should very much like to see the girl and the abbe too, whom she pitied, though she admitted he was to be blamed for what he had done. I had got her a dress to wear at dinner, which became her exquisitely. I felt only too happy to be able to please her in any way, for her conduct towards myself and the way she treated her ardent lover commanded my admiration. She saw him every day either at my house or at Rosalie's. The young man had received an excellent education, though he was of the mercantile class, and wrote to her in a business-like manner, that, as they were well suited to each other in every way, there was nothing against his going to Marseilles and obtaining her father's consent to the match, unless it were a feeling of aversion on her side. He finished by requesting her to give him an answer. She shewed me the letter, and I congratulated her, and advised her to accept, if there was nothing about the young man which displeased her.

"There is nothing of the kind," she said, "and Rosalie thinks with you."

"Then tell him by word of mouth that you give your consent, and will expect to see him at Marseilles."

"Very good; as you think so, I will tell him tomorrow."

When dinner was over a feeling of curiosity made me go into the room where Annette was dining with the Venetian girl, whose name was Marcoline. I was struck with astonishment on seeing her, for she was completely changed, not so much by the pretty dress she had on as by the contented expression of her face, which made her look quite another person. Good humour had vanquished unbecoming rage, and the gentleness born of happiness made her features breathe forth love. I could scarcely believe that this charming creature before me was the same who had dealt such a vigorous blow to my brother, a priest, and a sacred being in the eyes of the common people. They were eating, and laughing at not being able to understand each other, for Marcoline only spoke Venetian, and Annette Genoese, and the latter dialect does not resemble the former any more than Bohemian resembles Dutch.

I spoke to Marcoline in her native tongue, which was mine too, and she said,—

"I seem to have suddenly passed from hell to Paradise."

"Indeed, you look like an angel."

"You called me a little devil this morning. But here is a fair angel," said she, pointing to Annette; "we don't see such in Venice."

"She is my treasure."

Shortly after my niece came in, and seeing me talking and laughing with the two girls began to examine the new-comer. She told me in French that she thought her perfectly beautiful, and repeating her opinion to the girl in Italian gave her a kiss. Marcoline asked her plainly in the Venetian manner who she was.

"I am this gentleman's niece, and he is taking me back to Marseilles, where my home is."

"Then you would have been my niece too, if I had married his brother. I wish I had such a pretty niece."

This pleasant rejoinder was followed by a storm of kisses given and returned with ardour which one might pronounce truly Venetian, if it were not that this would wound the feelings of the almost equally ardent Provencals.

I took my niece for a sail in the bay, and after we had enjoyed one of those delicious evenings which I think can be found nowhere else—sailing on a mirror silvered by the moon, over which float the odours of the jasmine, the orange-blossom, the pomegranates, the aloes, and all the scented flowers which grow along the coasts—we returned to our lodging, and I asked Annette what had become of Marcoline. She told me that she had gone to bed early, and I went gently into her room, with no other intention than to see her asleep. The light of the candle awoke her, and she did not seem at all frightened at seeing me. I sat by the bed, and fell to making love to her, and at last made as if I would kiss her, but she resisted, and we went on talking.

When Annette had put her mistress to bed, she came in and found us together.

"Go to bed, my dear," said I. "I will come to you directly."

Proud of being my mistress, she gave me a fiery kiss and went away without a word.

I began to talk about my brother, and passing from him to myself I told her of the interest I felt for her, saying that I would either have her taken to Venice, or bring her with me when I went to France.

"Do you want to marry me?"

"No, I am married already."

"That's a lie, I know, but it doesn't matter. Send me back to Venice, and the sooner the better. I don't want to be anybody's concubine."

"I admire your sentiments, my dear, they do you honour."

Continuing my praise I became pressing, not using any force, but those gentle caresses which are so much harder for a woman to resist than a violent attack. Marcoline laughed, but seeing that I persisted in spite of her resistance, she suddenly glided out of the bed and took refuge in my niece's room and locked the door after her. I was not displeased; the thing was done so easily and gracefully. I went to bed with Annette, who lost nothing by the ardour with which Marcoline had inspired me. I told her how she had escaped from my hands, and Annette was loud in her praises.

In the morning I got up early and went into my niece's room to enjoy the sight of the companion I had involuntarily given her, and the two girls were certainly a very pleasant sight. As soon as my niece saw me, she exclaimed,—

"My dear uncle, would you believe it? This sly Venetian has violated me."

Marcoline understood her, and far from denying the fact proceeded to give my niece fresh marks of her affection, which were well received, and from the movements of the sheets which covered them I could make a pretty good guess as to the nature of their amusement.

"This is a rude shock to the respect which your uncle has had for your prejudices," said I.

"The sports of two girls cannot tempt a man who has just left the arms of
Annette."

"You are wrong, and perhaps you know it, for I am more than tempted."

With these words I lifted the sheets of the bed. Marcoline shrieked but did not move, but my niece earnestly begged me to replace the bed-clothes. However, the picture before me was too charming to be concealed.

At this point Annette came in, and in obedience to her mistress replaced the coverlet over the two Bacchantes. I felt angry with Annette, and seizing her threw her on the bed, and then and there gave the two sweethearts such an interesting spectacle that they left their own play to watch us. When I had finished, Annette, who was in high glee; said I was quite right to avenge myself on their prudery. I felt satisfied with what I had done, and went to breakfast. I then dressed, and visited my brother.

"How is Marcoline?" said he, as soon as he saw me.

"Very well, and you needn't trouble yourself any more about her. She is well lodged, well dressed, and well fed, and sleeps with my niece's maid."

"I didn't know I had a niece."

"There are many things you don't know. In three or four days she will return to Venice."

"I hope, dear brother, that you will ask me to dine with you to-day."

"Not at all, dear brother. I forbid you to set foot in my house, where your presence would be offensive to Marcoline, whom you must not see any more."

"Yes, I will; I will return to Venice, if I have to hang for it."

"What good would that be? She won't have you."

"She loves me."

"She beats you."

"She beats me because she loves me. She will be as gentle as a lamb when she sees me so well dressed. You do not know how I suffer."

"I can partly guess, but I do not pity you, for you are an impious and cruel fool. You have broken your vows, and have not hesitated to make a young girl endure misery and degradation to satisfy your caprice. What would you have done, I should like to know, if I had given you the cold shoulder instead of helping you?"

"I should have gone into the street, and begged for my living with her."

"She would have beaten you, and would probably have appealed to the law to get rid of you."

"But what will you do for me, if I let her go back to Venice without following her."

"I will take you to France, and try to get you employed by some bishop."

"Employed! I was meant by nature to be employed by none but God."

"You proud fool! Marcoline rightly called you a whiner. Who is your God? How do you serve Him? You are either a hypocrite or an idiot. Do you think that you, a priest, serve God by decoying an innocent girl away from her home? Do you serve Him by profaning the religion you do not even understand? Unhappy fool! do you think that with no talent, no theological learning, and no eloquence, you can be a Protestant minister. Take care never to come to my house, or I will have you expelled from Genoa."

"Well, well, take me to Paris, and I will see what my brother Francis can do for me; his heart is not so hard as yours."

"Very good! you shall go to Paris, and we will start from here in three or four days. Eat and drink to your heart's content, but remain indoors; I will let you know when we are going. I shall have my niece, my secretary, and my valet with me. We shall travel by sea."

"The sea makes me sick."

"That will purge away some of your bad humours."

When I got home I told Marcoline what had passed between us.

"I hate him!" said she; "but I forgive him, since it is through him I know you."

"And I forgive him, too, because unless it had been for him I should never have seen you. But I love you, and I shall die unless you satisfy my desires."

"Never; for I know I should be madly in love with you, and then you would leave me, and I should be miserable again."

"I will never leave you."

"If you will swear that, take me into France and make me all your own. Here you must continue living with Annette; besides, I have got your niece to make love to."

The pleasant part of the affair was that my niece was equally taken with her, and had begged me to let her take meals with us and sleep with her. As I had a prospect of being at their lascivious play, I willingly consented, and henceforth she was always present at the table. We enjoyed her company immensely, for she told us side-splitting tales which kept us at table till it was time to go to Rosalie's, where my niece's adorer was certain to be awaiting us.

The next day, which was Holy Thursday, Rosalie came with us to see the processions. I had Rosalie and Marcoline with me, one on each arm, veiled in their mezzaros, and my niece was under the charge of her lover. The day after we went to see the procession called at Genoa Caracce, and Marcoline pointed out my brother who kept hovering round us, though he pretended not to see us. He was most carefully dressed, and the stupid fop seemed to think he was sure to find favour in Marcoline's eyes, and make her regret having despised him; but he was woefully deceived, for Marcoline knew how to manage her mezzaro so well that, though he was both seen and laughed at, the poor devil could not be certain that she had noticed him at all, and in addition the sly girl held me so closely by the arm that he must have concluded we were very intimate.

My niece and Marcoline thought themselves the best friends in the world, and could not bear my telling them that their amorous sports were the only reason for their attachment. They therefore agreed to abandon them as soon as we left Genoa, and promised that I should sleep between them in the felucca, all of us to keep our clothes on. I said I should hold them to their word, and I fixed our departure for Thursday. I ordered the felucca to be in readiness and summoned my brother to go on board.

It was a cruel moment when I left Annette with her mother. She wept so bitterly that all of us had to shed tears. My niece gave her a handsome dress and I thirty sequins, promising to come and see her again on my return from England. Possano was told to go on board with the abbe; I had provisioned the boat for three days. The young merchant promised to be at Marseilles, telling my niece that by the time he came everything would be settled. I was delighted to hear it; it assured me that her father would give her a kind reception. Our friends did not leave us till the moment we went on board.

The felucca was very conveniently arranged, and was propelled by the twelve oarsmen. On the deck there were also twenty-four muskets, so that we should have been able to defend ourselves against a pirate. Clairmont had arranged my carriage and my trunks so cleverly, that by stretching five mattresses over them we had an excellent bed, where we could sleep and undress ourselves in perfect comfort; we had good pillows and plenty of sheets. A long awning covered the deck, and two lanterns were hung up, one at each end. In the evening they were lighted and Clairmont brought in supper. I had warned my brother that at the slightest presumption on his part he should be flung into the sea, so I allowed him and Possano to sup with us.

I sat between my two nymphs and served the company merrily, first my niece, then Marcoline, then my brother, and finally Possano. No water was drunk at table, so we each emptied a bottle of excellent Burgundy, and when we had finished supper the rowers rested on their oars, although the wind was very light. I had the lamps put out and went to bed with my two sweethearts, one on each side of me.

The light of dawn awoke me, and I found my darlings still sleeping in the same position. I could kiss neither of them, since one passed for my niece, and my sense of humanity would not allow me to treat Marcoline as my mistress in the presence of an unfortunate brother who adored her, and had never obtained the least favour from her. He was lying near at hand, overwhelmed with grief and seasickness, and watching and listening with all his might for the amorous encounter he suspected us of engaging in. I did not want to have any unpleasantness, so I contented myself with gazing on them till the two roses awoke and opened their eyes.

When this delicious sight was over, I got up and found that we were only opposite Final, and I proceeded to reprimand the master.

"The wind fell dead at Savona, sir;" and all the seamen chorused his excuse.

"Then you should have rowed instead of idling."

"We were afraid of waking you. You shall be at Antibes by tomorrow."

After passing the time by eating a hearty meal, we took a fancy to go on shore at St. Remo. Everybody was delighted. I took my two nymphs on land, and after forbidding any of the others to disembark I conducted the ladies to an inn, where I ordered coffee.

A man accosted us, and invited us to come and play biribi at his house.

"I thought the game was forbidden in Genoa," said I. I felt certain that the players were the rascals whose bank I had broken at Genoa, so I accepted the invitation. My niece had fifty Louis in her purse, and I gave fifteen to Marcoline. We found a large assemblage, room was made for us, and I recognized the knaves of Genoa. As soon as they saw me they turned pale and trembled. I should say that the man with the bag was not the poor devil who had served me so well without wanting to.

"I play harlequin," said I.

"There isn't one."

"What's the bank?"

"There it is. We play for small stakes here, and those two hundred louis are quite sufficient. You can bet as low as you like, and the highest stake is of a louis."

"That's all very well, but my louis is full weight."

"I think ours are, too."

"Are you sure?"

"No."

"Then I won't play," said I, to the keeper of the rooms.

"You are right; bring the scales."

The banker then said that when play was over he would give four crowns of six livres for every louis that the company had won, and the matter was settled. In a moment the board was covered with stakes.

We each punted a louis at a time, and I and my niece lost twenty Louis, but Marcoline, who had never possessed two sequins in her life before, won two hundred and forty Louis. She played on the figure of an abbe which came out fifth twenty times. She was given a bag full of crown pieces, and we returned to the felucca.

The wind was contrary, and we had to row all night, and in the morning the sea was so rough that we had to put in at Mentone. My two sweethearts were very sick, as also my brother and Possano, but I was perfectly well. I took the two invalids to the inn, and allowed my brother and Possano to land and refresh themselves. The innkeeper told me that the Prince and Princess of Monaco were at Mentone, so I resolved to pay them a visit. It was thirteen years since I had seen the prince at Paris, where I had amused him and his mistress Caroline at supper. It was this prince who had taken me to see the horrible Duchess of Rufec; then he was unmarried, and now I met him again in his principality with his wife, of whom he had already two sons. The princess had been a Duchess de Borgnoli, a great heiress, and a delightful and pretty woman. I had heard all about her, and I was curious to verify the facts for myself.

I called on the prince, was announced, and after a long wait they introduced me to his presence. I gave him his title of highness, which I had never done at Paris, where he was not known under his full style and title. He received me politely, but with that coolness which lets one know that one is not an over-welcome visitor.

"You have put in on account of the bad weather, I suppose?" said he.

"Yes, prince, and if your highness will allow me I will spend the whole day in your delicious villa." (It is far from being delicious.)

"As you please. The princess as well as myself likes it better than our place at Monaco, so we live here by preference."

"I should be grateful if your highness would present me to the princess."

Without mentioning my name he ordered a page in waiting to present me to the princess.

The page opened the door of a handsome room and said, "The Princess," and left me. She was singing at the piano, but as soon as she saw me she rose and came to meet me. I was obliged to introduce myself, a most unpleasant thing, and no doubt the princess felt the position, for she pretended not to notice it, and addressed me with the utmost kindness and politeness, and in a way that shewed that she was learned in the maxims of good society. I immediately became very much at my ease, and proceeded in a lordly manner to entertain her with pleasant talk, though I said nothing about my two lady friends.

The princess was handsome, clever, and good-natured. Her mother, who knew that a man like the prince would never make her daughter happy, opposed the marriage, but the young marchioness was infatuated, and the mother had to give in when the girl said,—

"O Monaco O monaca." (Either Monaco or a convent.)

We were still occupied in the trifles which keep up an ordinary conversation, when the prince came in running after a waiting-maid, who was making her escape, laughing. The princess pretended not to see him, and went on with what she was saying. The scene displeased me, and I took leave of the princess, who wished me a pleasant journey. I met the prince as I was going out, and he invited me to come and see him whenever I passed that way.

"Certainly," said I; and made my escape without saying any more.

I went back to the inn and ordered a good dinner for three.

In the principality of Monaco there was a French garrison, which was worth a pension of a hundred thousand francs to the prince— a very welcome addition to his income.

A curled and scented young officer, passing by our room, the door of which was open, stopped short, and with unblushing politeness asked us if we would allow him to join our party. I replied politely, but coldly, that he did us honour—a phrase which means neither yes nor no; but a Frenchman who has advanced one step never retreats.

He proceeded to display his graces for the benefit of the ladies, talking incessantly, without giving them time to get in a word, when he suddenly turned to me and said that he wondered how it was that the prince had not asked me and my ladies to dinner. I told him that I had not said anything to the prince about the treasure I had with me.

I had scarcely uttered the words, when the kindly blockhead rose and cried enthusiastically,—

"Parbleu! I am no longer surprised. I will go and tell his highness, and
I shall soon have the honour of dining with you at the castle."

He did not wait to hear my answer, but went off in hot haste.

We laughed heartily at his folly, feeling quite sure that we should neither dine with him nor the prince, but in a quarter of an hour he returned in high glee, and invited us all to dinner on behalf of the prince.

"I beg you will thank his highness, and at the same time ask him to excuse us. The weather has improved, and I want to be off as soon as we have taken a hasty morsel."

The young Frenchman exerted all his eloquence in vain, and at length retired with a mortified air to take our answer to the prince.

I thought I had got rid of him at last, but I did not know my man. He returned a short time after, and addressing himself in a complacent manner to the ladies, as if I was of no more account, he told them that he had given the prince such a description of their charms that he had made up his mind to dine with them.

"I have already ordered the table to be laid for two more, as I shall have the honour of being of the party. In a quarter of an hour, ladies, the prince will be here."

"Very good," said I, "but as the prince is coming I must go to the felucca and fetch a capital pie of which the prince is very fond, I know. Come, ladies."

"You can leave them here, sir. I will undertake to keep them amused."

"I have no doubt you would, but they have some things to get from the felucca as well."

"Then you will allow me to come too."

"Certainly with pleasure."

As we were going down the stairs, I asked the innkeeper what I owed him.

"Nothing, sir, I have just received orders to serve you in everything, and to take no money from you."

"The prince is really magnificent!" During this short dialogue, the ladies had gone on with the fop. I hastened to rejoin them, and my niece took my arm, laughing heartily to hear the officer making love to Marcoline, who did not understand a word he said. He did not notice it in the least, for his tongue kept going like the wheel of a mill, and he did not pause for any answers.

"We shall have some fun at dinner," said my niece, "but what are we going to do on the felucca?"

"We are leaving. Say nothing."

"Leaving?"

"Immediately."

"What a jest! it is worth its weight in gold."

We went on board the felucca, and the officer, who was delighted with the pretty vessel, proceeded to examine it. I told my niece to keep him company, and going to the master, whispered to him to let go directly.

"Directly?"

"Yes, this moment."

"But the abbe and your secretary are gone for a walk, and two of my men are on shore, too."

"That's no matter; we shall pick them up again at Antibes; it's only ten leagues, and they have plenty of money. I must go, and directly. Make haste."

"All right."

He tripped the anchor, and the felucca began to swing away from the shore. The officer asked me in great astonishment what it meant.

"It means that I am going to Antibes and I shall be very glad to take you there for nothing."

"This is a fine jest! You are joking, surely?"

"Your company will be very pleasant on the journey."

"Pardieu! put me ashore, for with your leave, ladies, I cannot go to Antibes."

"Put the gentleman ashore," said I to the master, "he does not seem to like our company."

"It's not that, upon my honour. These ladies are charming, but the prince would think that I was in the plot to play this trick upon him, which you must confess is rather strong."

"I never play a weak trick."

"But what will the prince say?"

"He may say what he likes, and I shall do as I like."

"Well, it's no fault of mine. Farewell, ladies! farewell, sir!"

"Farewell, and you may thank the prince for me for paying my bill."

Marcoline who did not understand what was passing gazed in astonishment, but my niece laughed till her sides ached, for the way in which the poor officer had taken the matter was extremely comic.

Clairmont brought us an excellent dinner, and we laughed incessantly during its progress, even at the astonishment of the abbe and Possano when they came to the quay and found the felucca had flown. However, I was sure of meeting them again at Antibes, and we reached that port at six o'clock in the evening.

The motion of the sea had tired us without making us feel sick, for the air was fresh, and our appetites felt the benefits of it, and in consequence we did great honour to the supper and the wine. Marcoline whose stomach was weakened by the sickness she had undergone soon felt the effects of the Burgundy, her eyes were heavy, and she went to sleep. My niece would have imitated her, but I reminded her tenderly that we were at Antibes, and said I was sure she would keep her word. She did not answer me, but gave me her hand, lowering her eyes with much modesty.

Intoxicated with her submission which was so like love, I got into bed beside her, exclaiming,—

"At last the hour of my happiness has come!

"And mine too, dearest."

"Yours? Have you not continually repulsed me?"

"Never! I always loved you, and your indifference has been a bitter grief to me."

"But the first night we left Milan you preferred being alone to sleeping with me."

"Could I do otherwise without passing in your eyes for one more a slave to sensual passion than to love? Besides you might have thought I was giving myself to you for the benefits I had received; and though gratitude be a noble feeling, it destroys all the sweet delights of love. You ought to have told me that you loved me and subdued me by those attentions which conquer the hearts of us women. Then you would have seen that I loved you too, and our affection would have been mutual. On my side I should have known that the pleasure you had of me was not given out of a mere feeling of gratitude. I do not know whether you would have loved me less the morning after, if I had consented, but I am sure I should have lost your esteem."

She was right, and I applauded her sentiments, while giving her to understand that she was to put all notions of benefits received out of her mind. I wanted to make her see that I knew that there was no more need for gratitude on her side than mine.

We spent a night that must be imagined rather than described. She told me in the morning that she felt all had been for the best, as if she had given way at first she could never have made up her mind to accept the young Genoese, though he seemed likely to make her happy.

Marcoline came to see us in the morning, caressed us, and promised to sleep by herself the rest of the voyage.

"Then you are not jealous?" said I.

"No, for her happiness is mine too, and I know she will make you happy."

She became more ravishingly beautiful every day.

Possano and the abbe came in just as we were sitting down to table, and my niece having ordered two more plates I allowed them to dine with us. My brother's face was pitiful and yet ridiculous. He could not walk any distance, so he had been obliged to come on horseback, probably for the first time in his life.

"My skin is delicate," said he, "so I am all blistered. But God's will be done! I do not think any of His servants have endured greater torments than mine during this journey. My body is sore, and so is my soul."

So saying he cast a piteous glance at Marcoline, and we had to hold our sides to prevent ourselves laughing. My niece could bear it no more, and said,—

"How I pity you, dear uncle!"

At this he blushed, and began to address the most absurd compliments to her, styling her "my dear niece." I told him to be silent, and not to speak French till he was able to express himself in that equivocal language without making a fool of himself. But the poet Pogomas spoke no better than he did.

I was curious to know what had happened at Mentone after we had left, and
Pogomas proceeded to tell the story.

"When we came back from our walk we were greatly astonished not to find the felucca any more. We went to the inn, where I knew you had ordered dinner; but the inn-keeper knew nothing except that he was expecting the prince and a young officer to dine with you. I told him he might wait for you in vain, and just then the prince came up in a rage, and told the inn-keeper that now you were gone he might look to you for his payment. 'My lord,' said the inn-keeper, 'the gentleman wanted to pay me, but I respected the orders I had received from your highness and would not take the money.' At this the prince flung him a louis with an ill grace, and asked us who we were. I told him that we belonged to you, and that you had not waited for us either, which put us to great trouble. 'You will get away easily enough,' said he; and then he began to laugh, and swore the jest was a pleasant one. He then asked me who the ladies were. I told him that the one was your niece, and that I knew nothing of the other; but the abbe interfered, and said she was your cuisine. The prince guessed he meant to say 'cousin,' and burst out laughing, in which he was joined by the young officer. 'Greet him from me,' said he, as he went away, 'and tell him that we shall meet again, and that I will pay him out for the trick he has played me.' The worthy host laughed, too, when the prince had gone, and gave us a good dinner, saying that the prince's louis would pay for it all. When we had dined we hired two horses, and slept at Nice. In the morning we rode on again, being certain of finding you here." Marcoline told the abbe in a cold voice to take care not to tell anyone else that she was his cuisine, or his cousin, or else it would go ill with him, as she did not wish to be thought either the one or the other. I also advised him seriously not to speak French for the future, as the absurd way in which he had committed himself made everyone about him ashamed.

Just as I was ordering post-horses to take us to Fréjus, a man appeared, and told me I owed him ten louis for the storage of a carriage which I had left on his hands nearly three years ago. This was when I was taking Rosalie to Italy. I laughed, for the carriage itself was not worth five louis. "Friend," said I, "I make you a present of the article."

"I don't want your present. I want the ten louis you owe me."

"You won't get the ten louis. I will see you further first."

"We will see about that;" and so saying he took his departure.

I sent for horses that we might continue our journey.

A few moments after, a sergeant summoned me to the governor's presence. I followed him, and was politely requested to pay the ten louis that my creditor demanded. I answered that, in the agreement I had entered into for six francs a month, there was no mention of the length of the term, and that I did not want to withdraw my carriage.

"But supposing you were never to withdraw it?"

"Then the man could bequeath his claim to his heir."

"I believe he could oblige you to withdraw it, or to allow it to be sold to defray expenses."

"You are right, sir, and I wish to spare him that trouble. I make him a present of the carriage."

"That's fair enough. Friend, the carriage is yours."

"But sir," said the plaintiff, "it is not enough; the carriage is not worth ten louis, and I want the surplus."

"You are in the wrong. I wish you a pleasant journey, sir, and I hope you will forgive the ignorance of these poor people, who would like to shape the laws according to their needs."

All this trouble had made me lose a good deal of time, and I determined to put off my departure till the next day. However, I wanted a carriage for Possano and the abbe, and I got my secretary to buy the one I had abandoned for four louis. It was in a deplorable state, and I had to have it repaired, which kept us till the afternoon of the next day; however, so far as pleasure was concerned, the time was not lost.

CHAPTER III

My Arrival at Marseilles—Madame d'Urfe—My Niece Is
Welcomed by Madame Audibert I Get Rid of My Brother and
Possano—Regeneration—Departure of Madame d'Urfe—Marcoline
Remains Constant

My niece, now my mistress, grew more dear to me every day, and
I could not help trembling when I reflected that Marseilles would be
the tomb of our love. Though I could not help arriving there, I
prolonged my happiness as long as I could by travelling by short
stages. I got to Frejus in less than three hours, and stopped there,
and telling Possano and the abbe to do as they liked during our
stay, I ordered a delicate supper and choice wine for myself and
my nymphs. Our repast lasted till midnight, then we went to bed,
and passed the time in sweet sleep and sweeter pleasures. I made
the same arrangements at Lucca, Brignoles, and Aubayne, where
I passed the sixth and last night of happiness.

As soon as I got to Marseilles I conducted my niece to Madame
Audibert's, and sent Possano and my brother to the "Trieze
Cantons" inn, bidding them observe the strictest silence with
regard to me, for Madame d'Urfe had been awaiting me for three
weeks, and I wished to be my own herald to her.

It was at Madame Audibert's that my niece had met Croce. She
was a clever woman, and had known the girl from her childhood,
and it was through her that my niece hoped to be restored to her
father's good graces. We had agreed that I should leave my niece
and Marcoline in the carriage, and should interview Madame

Audibert, whose acquaintance I had made before, and with whom I could make arrangements for my niece's lodging till some arrangement was come to.

Madame Audibert saw me getting out of my carriage, and as she did not recognize me her curiosity made her come down and open the door. She soon recognized me, and consented to let me have a private interview with the best grace in the world.

I did not lose any time in leading up to the subject, and after I had given her a rapid sketch of the affair, how misfortune had obliged La Croix to abandon Mdlle. Crosin, how I had been able to be of service to her, and finally, how she had had the good luck to meet a wealthy and distinguished person, who would come to Marseilles to ask her hand in a fortnight, I concluded by saying that I should have the happiness of restoring to her hands the dear girl whose preserver I had been.

"Where is she?" cried Madame Audibert.

"In my carriage. I have lowered the blinds."

"Bring her in, quick! I will see to everything. Nobody shall know that she is in my house."

Happier than a prince, I made one bound to the carriage and, concealing her face with her cloak and hood, I led my niece to her friend's arms. This was a dramatic scene full of satisfaction for me. Kisses were given and received, tears of happiness and repentance shed, I wept myself from mingled feelings of emotion, happiness, and regret.

In the meanwhile Clairmont had brought up my niece's luggage, and I went away promising to return and see her another day.

I had another and as important an arrangement to conclude, I mean with respect to Marcoline. I told the postillions to take me to the worthy old man's where I had lodged Rosalie so pleasantly. Marcoline was weeping at this separation from her friend. I got down at the house, and made my bargain hastily. My new mistress was, I said, to be lodged, fed, and attended on as if she had been a princess. He shewed me the apartment she was to occupy; it was fit for a young marchioness, and he told me that she should be attended by his own niece, that she should not leave the house, and that nobody but myself should visit her.

Having made these arrangements I made the fair Venetian come in. I gave her the money she had won, which I had converted into gold and made up to a thousand ducats.

"You won't want it here," said I, "so take care of it. At Venice a thousand ducats will make you somebody. Do not weep, dearest, my heart is with you, and to-morrow evening I will sup with you."

The old man gave me the latch-key, and I went off to the "Treize Cantons." I was expected, and my rooms were adjacent to those occupied by
Madame d'Urfe.

As soon as I was settled, Bourgnole waited on me, and told me her mistress was alone and expecting me impatiently.

I shall not trouble my readers with an account of our interview, as it was only composed of Madame d'Urfe's mad flights of fancy, and of lies on my part which had not even the merit of probability. A slave to my life of happy profligacy, I profited by her folly; she would have found someone else to deceive her, if I had not done so, for it was really she who deceived herself. I naturally preferred to profit by her rather than that a stranger should do so; she was very rich, and I did myself a great deal of good, without doing anyone any harm. The first thing she asked me was, "Where is Querilinthos?" And she jumped with joy when I told her that he was under the same roof.

"'Tis he, then, who shall make me young again. So has my genius assured me night after night. Ask Paralis if the presents I have prepared are good enough for Semiramis to present to the head of the Fraternity of the Rosy Cross."

I did not know what these presents were, and as I could not ask to see them, I answered that, before consulting Paralis, it would be necessary to consecrate the gifts under the planetary hours, and that Querilinthos himself must not see them before the consecration. Thereupon she took me to her closet, and shewed me the seven packets meant for the Rosicrucian in the form of offerings to the seven planets.

Each packet contained seven pounds of the metal proper to the planet, and seven precious stones, also proper to the planets, each being seven carats in weight; there were diamonds, rubies, emeralds, sapphires, chrysolites, topazes, and opals.

I made up my mind that nothing of this should pass into the hands of the Genoese, and told the mad woman that we must trust entirely in Paralis for the method of consecration, which must be begun by our placing each packet in a small casket made on purpose. One packet, and one only, could be consecrated in a day, and it was necessary to begin with the sun. It was now Friday, and we should have to wait till Sunday, the day of the sun. On Saturday I had a box with seven niches made for the purpose.

For the purposes of consecration I spent three hours every day with Madame d'Urfe, and we had not finished till the ensuing Saturday. Throughout this week I made Possano and my brother take their meals with us, and as the latter did not understand a word the good lady said, he did not speak a word himself, and might have passed for a mute of the seraglio. Madame d'Urfe pronounced him devoid of sense, and imagined we were going to put the soul of a sylph into his body that he might engender some being half human, half divine.

It was amusing to see my brother's despair and rage at being taken for an idiot, and when he endeavoured to say something to spew that he was not one, she only thought him more idiotic than ever. I laughed to myself, and thought how ill he would have played the part if I had asked him to do it. All the same the rascal did not lose anything by his reputation, for Madame d'Urfe clothed him with a decent splendour that would have led one to suppose that the abbe belonged to one of the first families in France. The most uneasy guest at Madame d'Urfe's table was Possano, who had to reply to questions, of the most occult nature, and, not knowing anything about the subject, made the most ridiculous mistakes.

I brought Madame d'Urfe the box, and having made all the necessary arrangements for the consecrations, I received an order from the oracle to go into the country and sleep there for seven nights in succession, to abstain from intercourse with all mortal women, and to perform ceremonial worship to the moon every night, at the hour of that planet, in the open fields. This would make me fit to regenerate Madame d'Urfe myself in case Querilinthos, for some mystic reasons, might not be able to do so.

Through this order Madame d'Urfe was not only not vexed with me for sleeping away from the hotel, but was grateful for the pains I was taking to ensure the success of the operation.

The day after my arrival I called on Madame Audibert, and had the pleasure of finding my niece wail pleased with the efforts her friend was making in her favour. Madame Audibert had spoken to her father, telling him that his daughter was with her, and that she hoped to obtain his pardon and to return to his house, where she would soon become the bride of a rich Genoese, who wished to receive her from her father's hands. The worthy man, glad to find again the lost sheep, said he would come in two days and take her to her aunt, who had a house at St. Louis, two leagues from the town. She might then quietly await the arrival of her future husband, and avoid all occasion of scandal. My niece was surprised that her father had not yet received a letter from the young man, and I could see that she was anxious about it; but I comforted her and assured her that I would not leave Marseilles till I had danced at her wedding.

I left her to go to Marcoline, whom I longed to press to my heart. I found her in an ecstasy of joy, and she said that if she could understand what her maid said her happiness would be complete. I saw that her situation was a painful one, especially as she was a woman, but for the present I saw no way out of the difficulty; I should have to get an Italian-speaking servant, and this would have been a troublesome task. She wept with joy when I told her that my niece desired to be remembered to her, and that in a day she would be on her father's hearth. Marcoline had found out that she was not my real niece when she found her in my arms.

The choice supper which the old man had procured us, and which spewed he had a good memory for my favorite tastes, made me think of Rosalie. Marcoline heard me tell the story with great interest, and said that it seemed to her that I only went about to make unfortunate girls happy, provided I found them pretty.

"I almost think you are right," said I; "and it is certain that I have made many happy, and have never brought misfortune to any girl."

"God will reward you, my dear friend."

"Possibly I am not worth His taking the trouble!"

Though the wit and beauty of Marcoline had charmed me, her appetite charmed me still more; the reader knows that I have always liked women who eat heartily. And in Marseilles they make an excellent dish of a common fowl, which is often so insipid.

Those who like oil will get on capitally in Provence, for it is used in everything, and it must be confessed that if used in moderation it makes an excellent relish.

Marcoline was charming in bed. I had not enjoyed the Venetian vices for nearly eight years, and Marcoline was a beauty before whom Praxiteles would have bent the knee. I laughed at my brother for having let such a treasure slip out of his hands, though I quite forgave him for falling in love with her. I myself could not take her about, and as I wanted her to be amused I begged my kind old landlord to send her to the play every day, and to prepare a good supper every evening. I got her some rich dresses that she might cut a good figure, and this attention redoubled her affection for me.

The next day, which was the second occasion on which I had visited her, she told me that she had enjoyed the play though she could not understand the dialogues; and the day after she astonished me by saying that my brother had intruded himself into her box, and had said so many impertinent things that if she had been at Venice she would have boxed his ears.

"I am afraid," she added, "that the rascal has followed me here, and will be annoying me."

"Don't be afraid," I answered, "I will see what I can do."

When I got to the hotel I entered the abbe's room, and by Possano's bed I saw an individual collecting lint and various surgical instruments.

"What's all this? Are you ill?"

"Yes, I have got something which will teach me to be wiser for the future."

"It's rather late for this kind of thing at sixty."

"Better late than never."

"You are an old fool. You stink of mercury."

"I shall not leave my room."

"This will harm you with the marchioness, who believes you to be the greatest of adepts, and consequently above such weaknesses."

"Damn the marchioness! Let me be."

The rascal had never talked in this style before. I thought it best to conceal my anger, and went up to my brother who was in a corner of the room.

"What do you mean by pestering Marcoline at the theatre yesterday?"

"I went to remind her of her duty, and to warn her that I would not be her complaisant lover."

"You have insulted me and her too, fool that you are! You owe all to Marcoline, for if it had not been for her, I should never have given you a second glance; and yet you behave in this disgraceful manner."

"I have ruined myself for her sake, and I can never shew my face in
Venice again. What right have you to take her from me?"

"The right of love, blockhead, and the right of luck, and the right of the strongest! How is it that she is happy with me, and does not wish to leave me?"

"You have dazzled her."

"Another reason is that with you she was dying of misery and hunger."

"Yes, but the end of it will be that you will abandon her as you have done with many others, whereas I should have married her."

"Married her! You renegade, you seem to forget that you are a priest. I do not propose to part with her, but if I do I will send her away rich."

"Well, well, do as you please; but still I have the right to speak to her whenever I like."

"I have forbidden you to do so, and you may trust me when I tell you that you have spoken to her for the last time."

So saying I went out and called on an advocate. I asked him if I could have a foreign abbe, who was indebted to me, arrested, although I had no proof of the debt.

"You can do so, as he is a foreigner, but you will have to pay caution-money. You can have him put under arrest at his inn, and you can make him pay unless he is able to prove that he owes you nothing. Is the sum a large one?"

"Twelve louis."

"You must come with me before the magistrate and deposit twelve louis, and from that moment you will be able to have him arrested. Where is he staying?"

"In the same hotel as I am, but I do not wish to have him arrested there, so I will get him to the 'Ste. Baume,' and put him under arrest. Here are the twelve louis caution-money, so you can get the magistrate's order, and we will meet again to-morrow."

"Give me his name, and yours also."

I returned in haste to the "Treize Cantons," and met the abbe, dressed up to the nines, and just about to go out.

"Follow me," said I, "I am going to take you to Marcoline, and you shall have an explanation in her presence."

"With pleasure."

He got into a carriage with me, and I told the coachman to take us to the "Ste. Baume" inn. When we got there, I told him to wait for me, that I was going to fetch Marcoline, and that I would return with her in a minute.

I got into the carriage again, and drove to the advocate, who gave the order for arrest to a policeman, who was to execute it. I then returned to the "Treize Cantons" and put his belongings into a trunk, and had them transported to his new abode.

I found him under arrest, and talking to the astonished host, who could not understand what it was all about. I told the landlord the mythical history of the abbe debt to me, and handed over the trunk, telling him that he had nothing to fear with regard to the bill, as I would take care that he should be well paid.

I then began my talk with the abbe, telling him that he must get ready to leave Marseilles the next day, and that I would pay for his journey to Paris; but that if he did not like to do so, I should leave him to his fate, and in three days he would be expelled from Marseilles. The coward began to weep and said he would go to Paris.

"You must start for Lyons to-morrow, but you will first write me out an I
O U for twelve louis."

"Why?"

"Because I say so. If you do so I will give you twelve louis and tear up the document before your face."

"I have no choice in the matter."

"You are right."

When he had written the I O U, I went to take a place in the diligence for him, and the next morning I went with the advocate to withdraw the arrest and to take back the twelve louis, which I gave to my brother in the diligence, with a letter to M. Bono, whom I warned not to give him any money, and to send him on to Paris by the same diligence. I then tore up his note of hand, and wished him a pleasant journey.

Thus I got rid of this foolish fellow, whom I saw again in Paris in a month's time.

The day I had my brother arrested and before I went to dine with Madame d'Urfe I had an interview with Possano in the hope of discovering the reason of his ill humour.

"The reason is," said he, "that I am sure you are going to lay hands on twenty or thirty thousand crowns in gold and diamonds, which the marchioness meant me to have."

"That may be, but it is not for you to know anything about it. I may tell you that it rests entirely with me to prevent your getting anything. If you think you can succeed go to the marchioness and make your complaints to her. I will do nothing to prevent you."

"Then you think I am going to help you in your imposture for nothing; you are very much mistaken. I want a thousand louis, and I will have it, too."

"Then get somebody to give it you," said I; and I turned my back on him.

I went up to the marchioness and told her that dinner was ready, and that we should dine alone, as I had been obliged to send the abbe away.

"He was an idiot; but how about Querilinthos?"

"After dinner Paralis will tell us all about him. I have strong suspicions that there is something to be cleared up."

"So have I. The man seems changed. Where is he?"

"He is in bed, ill of a disease which I dare not so much as name to you."

"That is a very extraordinary circumstance; I have never heard of such a thing before. It must be the work of an evil genius."

"I have never heard of such a thing, either; but now let us dine. We shall have to work hard to-day at the consecration of the tin."

"All the better. We must offer an expiatory sacrifice to Oromasis, for, awful thought! in three days he would have to regenerate me, and the operation would be performed in that condition."

"Let us eat now," I repeated; "I fear lest the hour of Jupiter be over-past."

"Fear nothing, I will see that all goes well."

After the consecration of the tin had been performed, I transferred
that of Oromasis to another day, while I consulted the oracle
assiduously, the marchioness translating the figures into letters.
The oracle declared that seven salamanders had transported the
true Querilinthos to the Milky Way, and that the man in the next
room was the evil genius, St. Germain, who had been put in that
fearful condition by a female gnome, who had intended to make
him the executioner of Semiramis, who was to die of the dreadful
malady before her term had expired. The oracle also said that
Semiramis should leave to Payaliseus Galtinardus (myself) all
the charge of getting rid of the evil genius, St. Germain; and that
she was not to doubt concerning her regeneration, since the word
would be sent me by the true Querilinthos from the Milky Way
on the seventh night of my worship of the moon. Finally the oracle
declared that I was to embrace Semiramis two days before the end
of the ceremonies, after an Undine had purified us by bathing us
in the room where we were.

I had thus undertaken to regenerate the worthy Semiramis, and I
began to think how I could carry out my undertaking without
putting myself to shame. The marchioness was handsome but old,
and I feared lest I should be unable to perform the great act. I was
thirty-eight, and I began to feel age stealing on me. The Undine,
whom I was to obtain of the moon, was none other than Marcoline,
who was to give me the necessary generative vigour by the sight of
her beauty and by the contact of her hands. The reader will see how
I made her come down from heaven.

I received a note from Madame Audibert which made me call on
her before paying my visit to Marcoline. As soon as I came in she

told me joyously that my niece's father had just received a letter from the father of the Genoese, asking the hand of his daughter for his only son, who had been introduced to her by the Chevalier de Seingalt, her uncle, at the Paretti's.

"The worthy man thinks himself under great obligations to you," said Madame Audibert. "He adores his daughter, and he knows you have cared for her like a father. His daughter has drawn your portrait in very favourable colors, and he would be extremely pleased to make your acquaintance. Tell me when you can sup with me; the father will be here to meet you, though unaccompanied by his daughter."

"I am delighted at what you tell me, for the young man's esteem for his future wife will only be augmented when he finds that I am her father's friend. I cannot come to supper, however; I will be here at six and stop till eight."

As the lady left the choice of the day with me I fixed the day after next, and then I repaired to my fair Venetian, to whom I told my news, and how I had managed to get rid of the abbe.

On the day after next, just as we were sitting down to dinner, the marchioness smilingly gave me a letter which Possano had written her in bad but perfectly intelligible French. He had filled eight pages in his endeavour to convince her that I was deceiving her, and to make sure he told the whole story without concealing any circumstance to my disadvantage. He added that I had brought two girls with me to Marseilles; and though he did not know where I had hidden them, he was sure that it was with them that I spent my nights.

After I had read the whole letter through, with the utmost coolness I gave it back to her, asking her if she had had the patience to read it through. She replied that she had run through it, but that she could not make it out at all, as the evil genius seemed to write a sort of outlandish dialect, which she did not care to puzzle herself over, as he could only have written down lies calculated to lead her astray at the most important moment of her life. I was much pleased with the marchioness's prudence, for it was important that she should have no suspicions about the Undine, the sight and the touch of whom were necessary to me in the great work I was about to undertake.

After dining, and discharging all the ceremonies and oracles which were necessary to calm the soul of my poor victim, I went to a banker and got a bill of a hundred louis on Lyons, to the order of M. Bono, and I advised him of what I had done, requesting him to cash it for Possano if it were presented on the day named thereon.

I then wrote the advice for Possano to take with him, it ran as follows: "M. Bonno, pay to M. Possano, on sight, to himself, and not to order, the sum of one hundred louis, if these presents are delivered to you on the 30th day of April, in the year 1763; and after the day aforesaid my order to become null and void."

With this letter in my hand I went to the traitor who had been lanced an hour before.

"You're an infamous traitor," I began, "but as Madame d'Urfe knows of the disgraceful state you are in she would not so much as read your letter. I have read it, and by way of reward I give you two alternatives which you must decide on immediately. I am in a hurry. You will either go to the hospital—for we can't have pestiferous fellows like you here—or start for Lyons in an hour. You must not stop on the way, for I have only given you sixty hours, which is ample to do forty posts in. As soon as you get to Lyons present this to M. Bono, and he will give you a hundred louis. This is a present from me, and afterwards I don't care what you do, as you are no longer in my service. You can have the carriage I bought for you at Antibes, and there is twenty-five louis for the journey: that is all. Make your choice, but I warn you that if you go to the hospital.I shall only give you a month's wages, as I dismiss you from my service now at this instant."

After a moment's reflection he said he would go to Lyons, though it would be at the risk of his life, for he was very ill.

"You must reap the reward of your treachery," said I, "and if you die it will be a good thing for your family, who will come in for what I have given you, but not what I should have given you if you had been a faithful servant."

I then left him and told Clairmont to pack up his trunk. I warned the inn-keeper of his departure and told him to get the post horses ready as soon as possible.

I then gave Clairmont the letter to Bono and twenty-five Louis, for him to hand them over to Possano when he was in the carriage and ready to go off.

When I had thus successfully accomplished my designs by means of the all-powerful lever, gold, which I knew how to lavish in time of need, I was once more free for my amours. I wanted to instruct the fair Marcoline, with whom I grew more in love every day. She kept telling me that her happiness would be complete if she knew French, and if she had the slightest hope that I would take her to England with me.

I had never flattered her that my love would go as far as that, but yet I could not help feeling sad at the thought of parting from a being who seemed made to taste voluptuous pleasures, and to communicate them with tenfold intensity to the man of her choice. She was delighted to hear that I had got rid of my two odious companions, and begged me to take her to the theatre, "for," said she, "everybody is asking who and what I am, and my landlord's niece is quite angry with me because I will not let her tell the truth."

I promised I would take her out in the course of the next week, but that for the present I had a most important affair on hand, in which I had need of her assistance.

"I will do whatever you wish, dearest."

"Very good! then listen to me. I will get you a disguise which will make you look like a smart footman, and in that costume you will call on the marchioness with whom I live, at the hour I shall name to you, and you will give her a note. Have you sufficient courage for that?"

"Certainly. Will you be there?"

"Yes. She will speak, but you must pretend to be dumb, as the note you bring with you will tell us; as also that you have come to wait upon us while we are bathing. She will accept the offer, and when she tells you to undress her from head to foot you will do so. When you have done, undress yourself, and gently rub the marchioness from the feet to the waist, but not higher. In the meanwhile I shall have taken off my clothes, and while I hold her in a close embrace you must stand so that I can see all your charms.

"Further, sweetheart, when I leave you you must gently wash her generative organs, and afterwards wipe them with a fine towel. Then do the same to me, and try to bring me to life again. I shall proceed to embrace the marchioness a second time, and when it is over wash her again and embrace her, and then come and embrace me and kiss in your Venetian manner the instrument with which the sacrifice is consummated. I shall then clasp the marchioness to my arms a third time, and you must caress us till the act is complete. Finally, you will wash us for the third time, then dress, take what she gives you and come here, where I will meet you in the course of an hour."

"You may reckon on my following all your instructions, but you must see that the task will be rather trying to my feelings."

"Not more trying than to mine. I could do nothing with the old woman if you were not present."

"Is she very old?"

"Nearly seventy."

"My poor sweetheart! I do pity you. But after this painful duty is over you must sup here and sleep with me."

"Certainly."

On the day appointed I had a long and friendly interview with the father of my late niece. I told him all about his daughter, only suppressing the history of our own amours, which were not suitable for a father's ears. The worthy man embraced me again and again, calling me his benefactor, and saying that I had done more for his daughter than he would have done himself, which in a sense was perhaps true. He told me that he had received another letter from the father, and a letter from the young man himself, who wrote in the most tender and respectful manner possible.

"He doesn't ask anything about the dower," said he, "a wonderful thing these days, but I will give her a hundred and fifty thousand francs, for the marriage is an excellent one, above all after my poor simpleton's escape. All Marseilles knows the father of her future husband, and to-morrow I mean to tell the whole story to my wife, and I am sure she will forgive the poor girl as I have done."

I had to promise to be present at the wedding, which was to be at Madame Audibert's. That lady knowing me to be very fond of play, and there being a good deal of play going on at her house, wondered why she did not see more of me; but I was at Marseilles to create and not to destroy: there is a time for everything.

I had a green velvet jacket made for Marcoline, with breeches of the same and silver-lace garters, green silk stockings, and fine leather shoes of the same colour. Her fine black hair was confined in a net of green silk, with a silver brooch. In this dress the voluptuous and well-rounded form of Marcoline was displayed to so much advantage, that if she had shewn herself in the street all Marseilles would have run after her, for, in spite of her man's dress, anybody could see that she was a girl. I took her to my rooms in her ordinary costume, to shew her where she would have to hide after the operation was over.

By Saturday we had finished all the consecrations, and the oracle fixed the regeneration of Semiramis for the following Tuesday, in the hours of the sun, Venus, and Mercury, which follow each other in the planetary system of the magicians, as also in Ptolemy's. These hours were in ordinary parlance the ninth, tenth, and eleventh of the day, since the day being a Tuesday, the first hour was sacred to Mars. And as at the beginning of May the hours are sixty-five minutes long, the reader, however little of a magician he may be, will understand that I had to perform the great work on Madame d'Urfe, beginning at half-past two and ending at five minutes to six. I had taken plenty of time, as I expected I should have great need of it.

On the Monday night, at the hour of the moon, I had taken Madame d'Urfe to the sea-shore, Clairmont following behind with the box containing the offerings, which weighed fifty pounds.

I was certain that nobody could see us, and I told my companion that the time was come. I told Clairmont to put down the box beside us, and to go and await us at the carriage. When we were alone we addressed a solemn prayer to Selenis, and then to the great satisfaction of the marchioness the box was consigned to the address. My satisfaction however was still greater than hers, for the box contained fifty pounds of lead. The real box, containing the treasure, was comfortably hidden in my room.

When we got back to the "Treize Cantons," I left Madame d'Urfe alone, telling her that I would return to the hotel when I had performed my conjurations to the moon, at the same hour and in the same place in which I had performed the seven consecrations.

I spoke the truth. I went to Marcoline, and while she was putting on her disguise I wrote on a sheet of white paper, in large and odd-looking letters, the following sentences, using, instead of ink, rock-alum:

"I am dumb but not deaf. I am come from the Rhone to bathe you. The hour of Oromasis has begun."

"This is the note you are to give to the marchioness," I said, "when you appear before her."

After supper we walked to the hotel and got in without anyone seeing us. I hid Marcoline in a large cupboard, and then putting on my dressing-gown I went to the marchioness to inform her that Selenis had fixed the next day for the hour of regeneration, and that we must be careful to finish before the hour of the moon began, as otherwise the operation would be annulled or at least greatly enfeebled.

"You must take care," I added, "that the bath be here beside your bed, and that Brougnole does not interrupt us."

"I will tell her to go out. But Selenis promised to send an Undine."

"True, but I have not yet seen such a being."

"Ask the oracle."

"Willingly."

She herself asked the question imploring Paralis not to delay the time of her regeneration, even though the Undine were lacking, since she could very well bathe herself.

"The commands of Oromasis change not," came the reply; "and in that you have doubted them you have sinned."

At this the marchioness arose and performed an expiatory sacrifice, and it appeared, on consulting the oracle, that Oromasis was satisfied.

The old lady did not move my pity so much as my laughter. She solemnly embraced me and said,—

"To-morrow, Galtinardus, you will be my spouse and my father." When I got back to my room and had shut the door, I drew the Undine out of her place of concealment. She undressed, and as she knew that I should be obliged to husband my forces, she turned her back on me, and we passed the night without giving each other a single kiss, for a spark would have set us all ablaze.

Next morning, before summoning Clairmont, I gave her her breakfast, and then replaced her in the cupboard. Later on, I gave her her instructions over again, telling her to do everything with calm precision, a cheerful face, and, above all, silence.

"Don't be afraid," said she, "I will make no mistakes."

As we were to dine at noon exactly, I went to look for the marchioness, but she was not in her room, though the bath was there, and the bed which was to be our altar was prepared.

A few moments after, the marchioness came out of her dressing-room, exquisitely painted, her hair arranged with the choicest lace, and looking radiant. Her breasts, which forty years before had been the fairest in all France, were covered with a lace shawl, her dress was of the antique kind, but of extremely rich material, her ear-rings were emeralds, and a necklace of seven aquamarines of the finest water, from which hung an enormous emerald, surrounded by twenty brilliants, each weighing a carat and a half, completed her costume. She wore on her finger the carbuncle which she thought worth a million francs, but which was really only a splendid imitation.

Seeing Semiramis thus decked out for the sacrifice, I thought it my bounden duty to offer her my homage. I would have knelt before her and kissed her hand, but she would not let me, and instead opened her arms and strained me to her breast.

After telling Brougnole that she could go out till six o'clock, we talked over our mysteries till the dinner was brought in.

Clairmont was the only person privileged to see us at dinner, at which Semiramis would only eat fish. At half-past one I told Clairmont I was not at home to anyone, and giving him a louis I told him to go and amuse himself till the evening.

The marchioness began to be uneasy, and I pretended to be so, too. I looked at my watch, calculated how the planetary hours were proceeding, and said from time to time,—

"We are still in the hour of Mars, that of the sun has not yet commenced."

At last the time-piece struck half-past two, and in two minutes afterwards the fair and smiling Undine was seen advancing into the room. She came along with measured steps, and knelt before Madame d'Urfe, and gave her the paper she carried. Seeing that I did not rise, the marchioness remained seated, but she raised the spirit with a gracious air and took the paper from her. She was surprised, however, to find that it was all white.

I hastened to give her a pen to consult the oracle on the subject, and after I had made a pyramid of her question, she interpreted it and found the answer:

"That which is written in water must be read in water."

"I understand now," said she, and going to the bath she plunged the paper into it, and then read in still whiter letters: "I am dumb, but not deaf. I am come from the Rhone to bathe you. The hour of Oromasis has begun."

"Then bathe me, divine being," said Semiramis, putting down the paper and sitting on the bed.

With perfect exactitude Marcoline undressed the marchioness, and delicately placed her feet in the water, and then, in a twinkling she had undressed herself, and was in the bath, beside Madame d'Urfe. What a contrast there was between the two bodies; but the sight of the one kindled the flame which the other was to quench.

As I gazed on the beautiful girl, I, too, undressed, and when I was ready to take off my shirt I spoke as follows: "O divine being, wipe the feet of Semiramis, and be the witness of my union with her, to the glory of the immortal Horomadis, King of the Salamanders."

Scarcely had I uttered my prayer when it was granted, and I consummated my first union with Semiramis, gazing on the charms of Marcoline, which I had never seen to such advantage before.

Semiramis had been handsome, but she was then what I am now, and without the Undine the operation would have failed. Nevertheless, Semiramis was affectionate, clean, and sweet in every respect, and had nothing disgusting about her, so I succeeded.

When the milk had been poured forth upon the altar, I said,—

"We must now await the hour of Venus."

The Undine performed the ablutions, embraced the bride, and came to perform the same office for me.

Semiramis was in an ecstasy of happiness, and as she pointed out to me the beauties of the Undine I was obliged to confess that I had never seen any mortal woman to be compared to her in beauty. Semiramis grew excited by so voluptuous a sight, and when the hour of Venus began I proceeded to the second assault, which would be the severest, as the hour was of sixty-five minutes. I worked for half an hour, steaming with perspiration, and tiring Semiramis, without being able to come to the point. Still I was ashamed to trick her. She, the victim, wiped the drops of sweat from my forehead, while the Undine, seeing my exhaustion, kindled anew the flame which the contact of that aged body had destroyed. Towards the end of the hour, as I was exhausted and still unsuccessful, I was obliged to deceive her by making use of those movements which are incidental to success. As I went out of the battle with all the signs of my strength still about me, Semiramis could have no doubts as to the reality of my success, and even the Undine was deceived when she came to wash me. But the third hour had come, and we were obliged to satisfy Mercury. We spent a quarter of the time in the bath, while the Undine delighted Semiramis by caresses which would have delighted the regent of France, if he had ever known of them. The good marchioness, believing these endearments to be peculiar to river spirits, was pleased with everything, and begged the Undine to shew me the same kindness. Marcoline obeyed, and lavished on me all the resources of the Venetian school of love. She was a perfect Lesbian, and her caresses having soon restored me to all my vigour I was encouraged to undertake to satisfy Mercury. I proceeded to the work, but alas! it was all in vain. I saw how my fruitless efforts vexed the Undine, and perceiving that Madame d'Urfe had had enough, I again took the course of deceiving her by pretended ecstacies and movements, followed by complete rest. Semiramis afterwards told me that my exertions shewed that I was something more than mortal.

I threw myself into the bath, and underwent my third ablution, then I dressed. Marcoline washed the marchioness and proceeded to clothe her, and did so with such a graceful charm that Madame d'Urfe followed the inspiration of her good genius, and threw her magnificent necklace over the Undine's neck. After a parting Venetian kiss she vanished, and went to her hiding place in the cupboard.

Semiramis asked the oracle if the operation had been successful. The answer was that she bore within her the seed of the sun, and that in the beginning of next February she would be brought to bed of another self of the same sex as the creator; but in order that the evil genii might not be able to do her any harm she must keep quiet in her bed for a hundred and seven hours in succession.

The worthy marchioness was delighted to receive this order, and looked upon it as a good omen, for I had tired her dreadfully. I kissed her, saying that I was going to the country to collect together what remained of the substances that I had used in my ceremonies, but I promised to dine with her on the morrow.

I shut myself up in my room with the Undine, and we amused ourselves as best we could till it was night, for she could not go out while it was light in her spiritual costume. I took off my handsome wedding garment, and as soon as it was dusk we crept out, and went away to Marcoline's lodging in a hackney coach, carrying with us the planetary offerings which I had gained so cleverly.

We were dying of hunger, but the delicious supper which was waiting for us brought us to life again. As soon as we got into the room Marcoline took off her green clothes and put on her woman's dress, saying,—

"I was not born to wear the breeches. Here, take the beautiful necklace the madwoman gave me!"

"I will sell it, fair Undine, and you shall have the proceeds."

"Is it worth much?"

"At least a thousand sequins. By the time you get back to Venice you will be worth at least five thousand ducats, and you will be able to get a husband and live with him in a comfortable style."

"Keep it all, I don't want it; I want you. I will never cease to love you; I will do whatever you tell me, and I promise never to be jealous. I will care for you—yes, as if you were my son."

"Do not let us say anything more about it, fair Marcoline, but let us go to bed, for you have never inspired me with so much ardour as now."

"But you must be tired."

"Yes, but not exhaustion, for I was only able to perform the distillation once."

"I thought you sacrificed twice on that old altar. Poor old woman! she is still pretty, and I have no doubt that fifty years ago she was one of the first beauties in France. How foolish of her to be thinking of love at that age."

"You excited me, but she undid your work even more quickly."

"Are you always obliged to have—a girl beside you when you make love to her?"

"No; before, there was no question of making a son."

"What? you are going to make her pregnant? That's ridiculous! Does she imagine that she has conceived?"

"Certainly; and the hope makes her happy."

"What a mad idea! But why did you try to do it three times?"

"I thought to shew my strength, and that if I gazed on you I should not fail; but I was quite mistaken."

"I pity you for having suffered so much."

"You will renew my strength."

As a matter of fact, I do not know whether to attribute it to the difference between the old and the young, but I spent a most delicious night with the beautiful Venetian—a night which I can only compare to those I passed at Parma with Henriette, and at Muran with the beautiful nun. I spent fourteen hours in bed, of which four at least were devoted to expiating the insult I had offered to love. When I had dressed and taken my chocolate I told Marcoline to dress herself with elegance, and to expect me in the evening just before the play began. I could see that she was intensely delighted with the prospect.

I found Madame d'Urfe in bed, dressed with care and in the fashion of a young bride, and with a smile of satisfaction on her face which I had never remarked there before.

"To thee, beloved Galtinardus, I owe all my happiness," said she, as she embraced me.

"I am happy to have contributed to it, divine Semiramis, but you must remember I am only the agent of the genii."

Thereupon the marchioness began to argue in the most sensible manner, but unfortunately the foundation of her argument was wholly chimerical.

"Marry me," said she; "you will then be able to be governor of the child, who will be your son. In this manner you will keep all my property for me, including what I shall have from my brother M. de Pontcarre, who is old and cannot live much longer. If you do not care for me in February next, when I shall be born again, into what hands shall I fall! I shall be called a bastard, and my income of twenty-four thousand francs will be lost to me. Think over it, dear Galtinardus. I must tell you that I feel already as if I were a man. I confess I am in love with the Undine, and I should like to know whether I shall be able to sleep with her in fourteen or fifteen years time. I shall be so if Oromasis will it, and then I shall be happy indeed. What a charming creature she is? Have you ever seen a woman like her? What a pity she is dumb!"

"She, no doubt, has a male water-spirit for a lover. But all of them are dumb, since it is impossible to speak in the water. I wonder she is not deaf as well. I can't think why you didn't touch her. The softness of her skin is something wonderful—velvet and satin are not to be compared to it! And then her breath is so sweet! How delighted I should be if I could converse with such an exquisite being."

"Dear Galtinardus, I beg you will consult the oracle to find out where I am to be brought to bed, and if you won't marry me I think I had better save all I have that I may have some provision when I am born again, for when I am born I shall know nothing, and money will be wanted to educate me. By selling the whole a large sum might be realized which could be put out at interest. Thus the interest would suffice without the capital being touched."

"The oracle must be our guide," said I. "You will be my son, and I will never allow anyone to call you a bastard."

The sublime madwoman was quiet by this assurance.

Doubtless many a reader will say that if I had been an honest man I should have undeceived her, but I cannot agree with them; it would have been impossible, and I confess that even if it had been possible I would not have done so, for it would only have made me unhappy.

I had told Marcoline to dress with elegance, and I put on one of my handsomest suits to accompany her to the theatre. Chance brought the two sisters Rangoni, daughters of the Roman consul, into our box. As I had made their acquaintance on my first visit to Marseilles, I introduced Marcoline to them as my niece, who only spoke Italian. As the two young ladies spoke the tongue of Tasso also, Marcoline was highly delighted. The younger sister, who was by far the handsomer of the two, afterwards became the wife of Prince Gonzaga Solferino. The prince was a cultured man, and even a genius, but very poor. For all that he was a true son of Gonzaga, being a son of Leopold, who was also poor, and a girl of the Medini family, sister to the Medini who died in prison at London in the year 1787.

Babet Rangoni, though poor, deserved to become a princess, for she had all the airs and manners of one. She shines under her name of Rangoni amongst the princess and princesses of the almanacs. Her vain husband is delighted at his wife being thought to belong to the illustrious family of Medini—an innocent feeling, which does neither good nor harm. The same publications turn Medini into Medici, which is equally harmless. This species of lie arises from the idiotic pride of the nobles who think themselves raised above the rest of humanity by their titles which they have often acquired by some act of baseness. It is of no use interfering with them on this point, since all things are finally appreciated at their true value, and the pride of the nobility is easily discounted when one sees them as they really are.

Prince Gonzaga Solferino, whom I saw at Venice eighteen years ago, lived on a pension allowed him by the empress. I hope the late emperor did not deprive him of it, as it was well deserved by this genius and his knowledge of literature.

At the play Marcoline did nothing but chatter with Babet Rangoni, who wanted me to bring the fair Venetian to see her, but I had my own reasons for not doing so.

I was thinking how I could send Madame d'Urfe to Lyons, for I had no further use for her at Marseilles, and she was often embarrassing. For instance, on the third day after her regeneration, she requested me to ask Paralis where she was to die—that is, to be brought to bed. I made the oracle reply that she must sacrifice to the water-spirits on the banks of two rivers, at the same hour, and that afterwards the question of her lying-in would be resolved. The oracle added that I must perform three expiatory sacrifices to Saturn, on account of my too harsh treatment of the false Querilinthos, and that Semiramis need not take part in these ceremonies, though she herself must perform the sacrifices to the water-spirits.

As I was pretending to think of a place where two rivers were sufficiently near to each other to fulfil the requirements of the oracle, Semiramis herself suggested that Lyons was watered by the Rhone and the Saone, and that it would be an excellent place for the ceremony. As may be imagined, I immediately agreed with her. On asking Paralis if there were any preparations to be made, he replied that it would be necessary to pour a bottle of sea-water into each river a fortnight before the sacrifice, and that this ceremony was to be performed by Semiramis in person, at the first diurnal hour of the moon.

"Then," said the marchioness, "the bottles must be filled here, for the other French ports are farther off. I will go as soon as ever I can leave my bed, and will wait for you at Lyons; for as you have to perform expiatory sacrifices to Saturn in this place, you cannot come with me."

I assented, pretending sorrow at not being able to accompany her. The next morning I brought her two well-sealed bottles of sea-water, telling her that she was to pour them out into the two rivers on the 15th of May (the current month). We fixed her departure for the 11th, and I promised to rejoin her before the expiration of the fortnight. I gave her the hours of the moon in writing, and also directions for the journey.

As soon as the marchioness had gone I left the "Treize Cantons" and went to live with Marcoline, giving her four hundred and sixty louis, which, with the hundred and forty she had won at biribi, gave her a total of six hundred louis, or fourteen thousand four hundred francs. With this sum she could look the future in the face fearlessly.

The day after Madame d'Urfe's departure, the betrothed of Mdlle. Crosin arrived at Marseilles with a letter from Rosalie, which he handed to me on the day of his arrival. She begged me in the name of our common honour to introduce the bearer in person to the father of the betrothed. Rosalie was right, but as the lady was not my real niece there were some difficulties in the way. I welcomed the young man and told him that I would first take him to Madame Audibert, and that we could then go together to his father-in-law in prospective.

The young Genoese had gone to the "Treize Cantons," where he thought I was staying. He was delighted to find himself so near the goal of his desires, and his ecstacy received a new momentum when he saw how cordially Madame Audibert received him. We all got into my carriage and drove to the father's who gave him an excellent reception, and then presented him to his wife, who was already friendly disposed towards him.

I was pleasantly surprised when this good and sensible man introduced me to his wife as his cousin, the Chevalier de Seingalt, who had taken such care of their daughter. The good wife and good mother, her husband's worthy partner, stretched out her hand to me, and all my trouble was over.

My new cousin immediately sent an express messenger to his sister, telling her that he and his wife, his future son-in-law, Madame Audibert, and a cousin she had not met before, would come and dine with her on the following day. This done he invited us, and Madame Audibert said that she would escort us. She told him that I had another niece with me, of whom his daughter was very fond, and would be delighted to see again. The worthy man was overjoyed to be able to increase his daughter's happiness.

I, too, was pleased with Madame Audibert's tact and thoughtfulness; and as making Marcoline happy was to make me happy also, I expressed my gratitude to her in very warm terms.

I took the young Genoese to the play, to Marcoline's delight, for she would have liked the French very much if she could have understood them. We had an excellent supper together, in the course of which I told Marcoline of the pleasure which awaited her on the morrow. I thought she would have gone wild with joy.

The next day we were at Madame Audibert's as punctually as Achilles on the field of battle. The lady spoke Italian well, and was charmed with Marcoline, reproaching me for not having introduced her before. At eleven we got to St. Louis, and my eyes were charmed with the dramatic situation. My late niece had an air of dignity which became her to admiration, and received her future husband with great graciousness; and then, after thanking me with a pleasant smile for introducing him to her father, she passed from dignity to gaiety, and gave her sweetheart a hundred kisses.

The dinner was delicious, and passed off merrily; but I alone preserved a tender melancholy, though I laughed to myself when they asked me why I was sad. I was thought to be sad because I did not talk in my usual vivacious manner, but far from being really sad that was one of the happiest moments of my life. My whole being was absorbed in the calm delight which follows a good action. I was the author of the comedy which promised such a happy ending. I was pleased with the thought that my influence in the world was more for good than for ill, and though I was not born a king yet I contrived to make many people happy. Everyone at table was indebted to me for some part of their happiness, and the father, the mother, and the betrothed pair wholly so. This thought made me feel a peaceful calm which I could only enjoy in silence.

Mdlle. Crosin returned to Marseilles with her father, her mother, and her future husband, whom the father wished to take up his abode with them. I went back with Madame Audibert, who made me promise to bring the delightful Marcoline to sup with her.

The marriage depended on the receipt of a letter from the young man's father, in answer to one from my niece's father. It will be taken for granted that we were all asked to the wedding, and Marcoline's affection for me increased every day.

When we went to sup with Madame Audibert we found a rich and witty young wine merchant at her house. He sat beside Marcoline, who entertained him with her sallies; and as the young man could speak Italian, and even the Venetian dialect (for he had spent a year at Venice), he was much impressed by the charms of my new niece.

I have always been jealous of my mistresses; but when a rival promises to marry them and give them a good establishment, jealousy gives way to a more generous feeling. For the moment I satisfied myself by asking Madame Audibert who he was, and I was delighted to hear that he had an excellent reputation, a hundred thousand crowns, a large business, and complete independence.

The next day he came to see us in our box at the theatre, and Marcoline received him very graciously. Wishing to push the matter on I asked him to sup with us, and when he came I was well pleased with his manners and his intelligence; to Marcoline he was tender but respectful. On his departure I told him I hoped he would come and see us again, and when we were alone I congratulated Marcoline on her conquest, and shewed her that she might succeed almost as well as Mdlle. Crosin. But instead of being grateful she was furiously, angry.

"If you want to get rid of me," said she, "send me back to Venice, but don't talk to me about marrying."

"Calm yourself, my angel! I get rid of you? What an idea! Has my behaviour led you to suppose that you are in my way? This handsome, well-educated, and rich young man has come under my notice. I see he loves you and you like him, and as I love you and wish to see you sheltered from the storms of fortune, and as I think this pleasant young Frenchman would make you happy, I have pointed out to you these advantages, but instead of being grateful you scold me. Do not weep, sweetheart, you grieve my very soul!"

"I am weeping because you think that I can love him."

"It might be so, dearest, and without my honour taking any hurt; but let us say no more about it and get into bed."

Marcoline's tears changed to smiles and kisses, and we said no more about the young wine merchant. The next day he came to our box again, but the scene had changed; she was polite but reserved, and I dared not ask him to supper as I had done the night before. When we had got home Marcoline thanked me for not doing so, adding that she had been afraid I would.

"What you said last night is a sufficient guide for me for the future."

In the morning Madame Audibert called on behalf of the wine merchant to ask us to sup with him. I turned towards the fair Venetian, and guessing my thoughts she hastened to reply that she would be happy to go anywhere in company with Madame Audibert. That lady came for us in the evening, and took us to the young man's house, where we found a magnificent supper, but no other guests awaiting us. The house was luxuriously furnished, it only lacked a mistress. The master divided his attention between the two ladies, and Marcoline looked ravishing. Everything convinced me that she had kindled the ardour of the worthy young wine merchant.

The next day I received a note from Madame Audibert, asking me to call on her. When I went I found she wanted to give my consent to the marriage of Marcoline with her friend.

"The proposal is a very agreeable one to me," I answered, "and I would willingly give her thirty thousand francs as a dowry, but I can have nothing to do with the matter personally. I will send her to you; and if you can win her over you may count on my word, but do not say that you are speaking on my behalf, for that might spoil everything."

"I will come for her, and if you like she shall dine with me, and you can take her to the play in the evening."

Madame Audibert came the following day, and Marcoline went to dinner with her. I called for her at five o'clock, and finding her looking pleased and happy I did not know what to think. As Madame Audibert did not take me aside I stifled my curiosity and went with Marcoline to the theatre, without knowing what had passed.

On the way Marcoline sang the praises of Madame Audibert, but did not say a word of the proposal she must have made to her. About the middle of the piece, however, I thought I saw the explanation of the riddle, for the young man was in the pit, and did not come to our box though there were two empty places.

We returned home without a word about the merchant or Madame Audibert, but as I knew in my own mind what had happened, I felt disposed to be grateful, and I saw that Marcoline was overjoyed to find me more affectionate than ever. At last, amidst our amorous assaults, Marcoline, feeling how dearly I loved her, told me what had passed between her and Madame Audibert.

"She spoke to me so kindly and so sensibly," said she, "but I contented myself with saying that I would never marry till you told me to do so. All the same I thank you with all my heart for the ten thousand crowns you are willing to give me. You have tossed the ball to me and I have sent it back. I will go back to Venice whenever you please if you will not take me to England with you, but I will never marry. I expect we shall see no more of the young gentleman, though if I had never met you I might have loved him."

It was evidently all over, and I liked her for the part she had taken, for a man who knows his own worth is not likely to sigh long at the feet of an obdurate lady.

The wedding-day of my late niece came round. Marcoline was there, without diamonds, but clad in a rich dress which set off her beauty and satisfied my vanity.

CHAPTER IV

I Leave Marseilles—Henriette at Aix—Irene at Avignon—Treachery of Possano—Madame d'Urfe Leaves Lyon

The wedding only interested me because of the bride. The plentiful rather than choice repast, the numerous and noisy company, the empty compliments, the silly conversation, the roars of laughter at very poor jokes—all this would have driven me to despair if it had not been for Madame Audibert, whom I did not leave for a moment. Marcoline followed the young bride about like a shadow, and the latter, who was going to Genoa in a week, wanted Marcoline to come in her train, promising to have her taken to Venice by a person of trust, but my sweetheart would listen to no proposal for separating her from me,—

"I won't go to Venice," she said, "till you send me there."

The splendours of her friend's marriage did not make her experience the least regret at having refused the young wine merchant. The bride beamed with happiness, and on my congratulating her she confessed her joy to be great, adding that it was increased by the fact that she owed it all to me. She was also very glad to be going to Genoa, where she was sure of finding a true friend in Rosalie, who would sympathize with her, their fortunes having been very similar.

The day after the wedding I began to make preparations for my departure. The first thing I disposed of was the box containing the planetary offerings. I kept the diamonds and precious stones, and took all the gold and silver to Rousse de Cosse, who still held the sum which Greppi had placed to my credit. I took a bill of exchange on Tourton and Bauer, for I should not be wanting any money at Lyons as Madame d'Urfe was there, and consequently the three hundred louis I had about me would be ample. I acted differently where Marcoline was concerned. I added a sufficient sum to her six hundred louis to give her a capital in round numbers of fifteen thousand francs. I got a bill drawn on Lyons for that amount, for I intended at the first opportunity to send her back to Venice, and with that idea had her trunks packed separately with all the linen and dresses which I had given her in abundance.

On the eve of our departure we took leave of the newly-married couple and the whole family at supper, and we parted with tears, promising each other a lifelong friendship.

The next day we set out intending to travel all night and not to stop till we got to Avignon, but about five o'clock the chain of the carriage broke, and we could go no further until a wheelwright had repaired the damage. We settled ourselves down to wait patiently, and Clairmont went to get information at a fine house on our right, which was approached by an alley of trees. As I had only one postillion, I did not allow him to leave his horses for a moment. Before long we saw Clairmont reappear with two servants, one of whom invited me, on behalf of his master, to await the arrival of the wheelwright at his house. It would have been churlish to refuse this invitation which was in the true spirit of French politeness, so leaving Clairmont in charge Marcoline and I began to wend our way towards the hospitable abode.

Three ladies and two gentleman came to meet us, and one of the gentlemen said they congratulated themselves on my small mishap, since it enabled madam to offer me her house and hospitality. I turned towards the lady whom the gentleman had indicated, and thanked her, saying, that I hoped not to trouble her long, but that I was deeply grateful for her kindness. She made me a graceful curtsy, but I could not make out her features, for a stormy wind was blowing, and she and her two friends had drawn their hoods almost entirely over their faces. Marcoline's beautiful head was uncovered and her hair streaming in the breeze. She only replied by graceful bows and smiles to the compliments which were addressed to her on all sides. The gentleman who had first accosted me asked me, as he gave her his arm, if she were my daughter. Marcoline smiled and I answered that she was my cousin, and that we were both Venetians.

A Frenchman is so bent on flattering a pretty woman that he will always do so, even if it be at the expense of a third party. Nobody could really think that Marcoline was my daughter, for though I was twenty years older than she was, I looked ten years younger than my real age, and so Marcoline smiled suggestively.

We were just going into the house when a large mastiff ran towards us, chasing a pretty spaniel, and the lady, being afraid of getting bitten, began to run, made a false step, and fell to the ground. We ran to help her, but she said she had sprained her ankle, and limped into the house on the arm of one of the gentlemen. Refreshments were brought in, and I saw that Marcoline looked uneasy in the company of a lady who was talking to her. I hastened to excuse her, saying that she did not speak French. As a matter of fact, Marcoline had begun to talk a sort of French, but the most charming language in the world will not bear being spoken badly, and I had begged her not to speak at all till she had learned to express herself properly. It is better to remain silent than to make strangers laugh by odd expressions and absurd equivocations.

The less pretty, or rather the uglier, of the two ladies said that it was astonishing that the education of young ladies was neglected in such a shocking manner at Venice. "Fancy not teaching them French!"

"It is certainly very wrong, but in my country young ladies are neither taught foreign languages nor round games. These important branches of education are attended to afterwards."

"Then you are a Venetian, too?"

"Yes, madam."

"Really, I should not have thought so."

I made a bow in return for this compliment, which in reality was only an insult; for if flattering to me it was insulting to the rest of my fellow-countrymen, and Marcoline thought as much for she made a little grimace accompanied by a knowing smile.

"I see that the young lady understands French," said our flattering friend, "she laughs exactly in the right place."

"Yes, she understands it, and as for her laughter it was due to the fact that she knows me to be like all other Venetians."

"Possibly, but it is easy to see that you have lived a long time in France."

"Yes, madam," said Marcoline; and these words in her pretty Venetian accent were a pleasure to hear.

The gentleman who had taken the lady to her room said that she found her foot to be rather swollen, and had gone to bed hoping we would all come upstairs.

We found her lying in a splendid bed, placed in an alcove which the thick curtains of red satin made still darker. I could not see whether she was young or old, pretty or ugly. I said that I was very sorry to be the indirect cause of her mishap, and she replied in good Italian that it was a matter of no consequence, and that she did not think she could pay too dear for the privilege of entertaining such pleasant guests.

"Your ladyship must have lived in Venice to speak the language with so much correctness."

"No, I have never been there, but I have associated a good deal with Venetians."

A servant came and told me that the wheelwright had arrived, and that he would take four hours to mend my carriage, so I went downstairs. The man lived at a quarter of a league's distance, and by tying the carriage pole with ropes, I could drive to his place, and wait there for the carriage to be mended. I was about to do so, when the gentleman who did the honours of the house came and asked me, on behalf of the lady, to sup and pass the night at her house, as to go to the wheelwright's would be out of my way; the man would have to work by night, I should be uncomfortable, and the work would be ill done. I assented to the countess's proposal, and having agreed with the man to come early the next day and bring his tools with him, I told Clairmont to take my belongings into the room which was assigned to me.

When I returned to the countess's room I found everyone laughing at Marcoline's sallies, which the countess translated. I was not astonished at seeing the way in which my fair Venetian caressed the countess, but I was enraged at not being able to see her, for I knew Marcoline would not treat any woman in that manner unless she were pretty.

The table was spread in the bedroom of the countess, whom I hoped to see at supper-time, but I was disappointed; for she declared that she could not take anything, and all supper-time she talked to Marcoline and myself, shewing intelligence, education, and a great knowledge of Italian. She let fall the expression, "my late husband," so I knew her for a widow, but as I did not dare to ask any questions, my knowledge ended at that point. When Clairmont was undressing me he told me her married name, but as I knew nothing of the family that was no addition to my information.

When we had finished supper, Marcoline took up her old position by the countess's bed, and they talked so volubly to one another that nobody else could get in a word.

When politeness bade me retire, my pretended cousin said she was going to sleep with the countess. As the latter laughingly assented, I refrained from telling my madcap that she was too forward, and I could see by their mutual embraces that they were agreed in the matter. I satisfied myself with saying that I could not guarantee the sex of the countess's bed-fellow, but she answered,

"Never mind; if there be a mistake I shall be the gainer."

This struck me as rather free, but I was not the man to be scandalized. I was amused at the tastes of my fair Venetian, and at the manner in which she contrived to gratify them as she had done at Genoa with my last niece. As a rule the Provencal women are inclined this way, and far from reproaching them I like them all the better for it.

The next day I rose at day-break to hurry on the wheelwright, and when the work was done I asked if the countess were visible. Directly after Marcoline came out with one of the gentlemen, who begged me to excuse the countess, as she could not receive me in her present extremely scanty attire; "but she hopes that whenever you are in these parts you will honour her and her house by your company, whether you are alone or with friends."

This refusal, gilded as it was, was a bitter pill for me to swallow, but I concealed my disgust, as I could only put it down to Marcoline's doings; she seemed in high spirits, and I did not like to mortify her. I thanked the gentleman with effusion, and placing a Louis in the hands of all the servants who were present I took my leave.

I kissed Marcoline affectionately, so that she should not notice my ill humour, and asked how she and the countess spent the night.

"Capitally," said she. "The countess is charming, and we amused ourselves all night with the tricks of two amorous women."

"Is she pretty or old?"

"She is only thirty-three, and, I assure you, she is as pretty as my friend Mdlle. Crosin. I can speak with authority for we saw each other in a state of nature."

"You are a singular creature; you were unfaithful to me for a woman, and left me to pass the night by myself."

"You must forgive me, and I had to sleep with her as she was the first to declare her love."

"Really? How was that?"

"When I gave her the first of my kisses she returned it in the Florentine manner, and our tongues met. After supper, I confess, I was the first to begin the suggestive caresses, but she met me half-way. I could only make her happy by spending the night with her. Look, this will shew you how pleased she was."

With these words Marcoline drew a superb ring, set with brilliants, from her finger. I was astonished.

"Truly," I said, "this woman is fond of pleasure and deserves to have it."

I gave my Lesbian (who might have vied with Sappho) a hundred kisses, and forgave her her infidelity.

"But," I remarked, "I can't think why she did not want me to see her; I think she has treated me rather cavalierly."

"No, I think the reason was that she was ashamed to be seen by my lover after having made me unfaithful to him; I had to confess that we were lovers."

"Maybe. At all events you have been well paid; that ring is worth two hundred louis."

"But I may as well tell you that I was well enough paid for the pleasure
I gave by the pleasure I received."

"That's right; I am delighted to see you happy."

"If you want to make me really happy, take me to England with you. My uncle will be there, and I could go back to Venice with him."

"What! you have an uncle in England? Do you really mean it? It sounds like a fairy-tale. You never told me of it before."

"I have never said anything about it up to now, because I have always imagined that this might prevent your accomplishing your desire."

"Is your uncle a Venetian? What is he doing in England? Are you sure that he will welcome you?"

"Yes."

"What is his name? And how are we to find him in a town of more than a million inhabitants?"

"He is ready found. His name is Mattio Boisi, and he is valet de chambre to M. Querini, the Venetian ambassador sent to England to congratulate the new king; he is accompanied by the Procurator Morosini. My uncle is my mother's brother; he is very fond of me, and will forgive my fault, especially when he finds I am rich. When he went to England he said he would be back in Venice in July, and we shall just catch him on the point of departure."

As far as the embassy went I knew it was all true, from the letters I had received from M. de Bragadin, and as for the rest Marcoline seemed to me to be speaking the truth. I was flattered by her proposal and agreed to take her to England so that I should possess her for five or six weeks longer without committing myself to anything.

We reached Avignon at the close of the day, and found ourselves very hungry. I knew that the "St. Omer" was an excellent inn, and when I got there I ordered a choice meal and horses for five o'clock the next morning. Marcoline, who did not like night travelling, was in high glee, and threw her arms around my neck, saying,—

"Are we at Avignon now?"

115

"Yes, dearest."

"Then I conscientiously discharge the trust which the countess placed in me when she embraced me for the last time this morning. She made me swear not to say a word about it till we got to Avignon."

"All this puzzles me, dearest; explain yourself."

"She gave me a letter for you."

"A letter?"

"Will you forgive me for not placing it in your hands sooner?"

"Certainly, if you passed your word to the countess; but where is this letter?"

"Wait a minute."

She drew a large bundle of papers from her pocket, saying,—

"This is my certificate of baptism."

"I see you were born in 1746."

"This is a certificate of 'good conduct.'"

"Keep it, it may be useful to you."

"This is my certificate of virginity."

"That's no use. Did you get it from a midwife?"

"No, from the Patriarch of Venice."

"Did he test the matter for himself?"

"No, he was too old; he trusted in me."

"Well, well, let me see the letter."

"I hope I haven't lost it."

"I hope not, to God."

"Here is your brother's promise of marriage; he wanted to be a Protestant."

"You may throw that into the fire."

"What is a Protestant?"

"I will tell you another time. Give me the letter."

"Praised be God, here it is!"

"That's lucky; but it has no address."

My heart beat fast, as I opened it, and found, instead of an address, these words in Italian:

"To the most honest man of my acquaintance."

Could this be meant for me? I turned down the leaf, and read one word—Henriette! Nothing else; the rest of the paper was blank.

At the sight of that word I was for a moment annihilated.

"Io non mori, e non rimasi vivo."

Henriette! It was her style, eloquent in its brevity. I recollected her last letter from Pontarlier, which I had received at Geneva, and which contained only one word—Farewell!

Henriette, whom I had loved so well, whom I seemed at that moment to love as well as ever. "Cruel Henriette," said I to myself, "you saw me and would not let me see you. No doubt you thought your charms would not have their old power, and feared lest I should discover that after all you were but mortal. And yet I love you with all the ardour of my early passion. Why did you not let me learn from your own mouth that you were happy? That is the only question I should have asked you, cruel fair one. I should not have enquired whether you loved me still, for I feel my unworthiness, who have loved other women after loving the most perfect of her sex. Adorable Henriette, I will fly to you to-morrow, since you told me that I should be always welcome."

I turned these thoughts over in my own mind, and fortified myself in this resolve; but at last I said,—

"No, your behaviour proves that you do not wish to see me now, and your wishes shall be respected; but I must see you once before I die."

Marcoline scarcely dared breathe to see me thus motionless and lost in thought, and I do not know when I should have come to myself if the landlord had not come in saying that he remembered my tastes, and had got me a delicious supper. This brought me to my senses, and I made my fair Venetian happy again by embracing her in a sort of ecstacy.

"Do you know," she said, "you quite frightened me? You were as pale and still as a dead man, and remained for a quarter of an hour in a kind of swoon, the like of which I have never seen. What is the reason? I knew that the countess was acquainted with you, but I should never have thought that her name by itself could have such an astonishing effect."

"Well, it is strange; but how did you find out that the countess knew me?"

"She told me as much twenty times over in the night, but she made me promise to say nothing about it till I had given you the letter."

"What did she say to you about me?"

"She only repeated in different ways what she has written for an address."

"What a letter it is! Her name, and nothing more."

"It is very strange."

"Yes, but the name tells all."

"She told me that if I wanted to be happy I should always remain with you. I said I knew that well; but that you wanted to send me back to Venice, though you were very fond of me. I can guess now that you were lovers. How long ago was it?"

"Sixteen or seventeen years."

"She must have been very young, but she cannot have been prettier than she is now."

"Be quiet, Marcoline."

"Did your union with her last long?"

"We lived together four months in perfect happiness."

"I shall not be happy for so long as that."

"Yes you will, and longer, too; but with another man, and one more suitable to you in age. I am going to England to try to get my daughter from her mother."

"Your daughter? The countess asked me if you were married, and I said no."

"You were right; she is my illegitimate daughter. She must be ten now, and when you see her you will confess that she must belong to me."

Just as we were sitting down to table we heard someone going downstairs to the table d'hote in the room where I had made Madame Stuard's acquaintance, our door was open, and we could see the people on the stairs; and one of them seeing us gave a cry of joy, and came running in, exclaiming, "My dear papa!" I turned to the light and saw Irene, the same whom I had treated so rudely at Genoa after my discussion with her father about biribi. I embraced her effusively, and the sly little puss, pretending to be surprised to see Marcoline, made her a profound bow, which was returned with much grace. Marcoline listened attentively to our conversation.

"What are you doing here, fair Irene?"

"We have been here for the last fortnight. Good heavens! how lucky I am to find you again. I am quite weak. Will you allow me to sit down, madam?"

"Yes, yes, my dear," said I, "sit down;" and I gave her a glass of wine which restored her.

A waiter came up, and said they were waiting for her at supper, but she said, "I won't take any supper;" and Marcoline, always desirous of pleasing me, ordered a third place to be laid. I made her happy by giving an approving nod.

We sat down to table, and ate our meal with great appetite. "When we have done," I said to Irene, "you must tell us what chance has brought you to Avignon."

Marcoline, who had not spoken a word hitherto, noticing how hungry Irene was, said pleasantly that it would have been a mistake if she had not taken any supper. Irene was delighted to hear Venetian spoken, and thanked her for her kindness, and in three or four minutes they had kissed and become friends.

It amused me to see the way in which Marcoline always fell in love with pretty women, just as if she had been a man.

In the course of conversation I found that Irene's father and mother were at the table d'hote below, and from sundry exclamations, such as "you have been brought to Avignon out of God's goodness," I learned that they were in distress. In spite of that Irene's mirthful countenance matched Marcoline's sallies, and the latter was delighted to hear that Irene had only called me papa because her mother had styled her my daughter at Milan.

We had only got half-way through our supper when Rinaldi and his wife came in. I asked them to sit down, but if it had not been for Irene I should have given the old rascal a very warm reception. He began to chide his daughter for troubling me with her presence when I had such fair company already, but Marcoline hastened to say that Irene could only have given me pleasure, for in my capacity of her uncle I was always glad when she was able to enjoy the society of a sweet young girl.

"I hope," she added, "that if she doesn't mind she will sleep with me."

"Yes, yes," resounded on all sides, and though I should have preferred to sleep with Marcoline by herself, I laughed and agreed; I have always been able to accommodate myself to circumstances.

Irene shared Marcoline's desires, for when it was settled that they should sleep together they seemed wild with joy, and I added fuel to the fire by plying them with punch and champagne.

Rinaldi and his wife did not leave us till they were quite drunk. When we had got rid of them, Irene told us how a Frenchman had fallen in love with her at Genoa, and had persuaded her father to go to Nice where high play was going on, but meeting with no luck there she had been obliged to sell what she had to pay the inn-keeper. Her lover had assured her that he would make it up to her at

Aix, where there was some money owing to him, and she persuaded her father to go there; but the persons who owed the money having gone to Avignon, there had to be another sale of goods.

"When we got here the luck was no better, and the poor young man, whom my father reproached bitterly, would have killed himself if I had not given him the mantle you gave me that he might pawn it and go on his quest. He got four louis for it, and sent me the ticket with a very tender letter, in which he assured me that he would find some money at Lyons, and that he would then return and take us to Bordeaux, where we are to find treasures. In the meanwhile we are penniless, and as we have nothing more to sell the landlord threatens to turn us out naked."

"And what does your father mean to do?"

"I don't know. He says Providence will take care of us."

"What does your mother say?"

"Oh! she was as quiet as usual."

"How about yourself?"

"Alas! I have to bear a thousand mortifications every day. They are continually reproaching me with having fallen in love with this Frenchman, and bringing them to this dreadful pass."

"Were you really in love with him?"

"Yes, really."

"Then you must be very unhappy."

"Yes, very; but not on account of my love, for I shall get over that in time, but because of that which will happen to-morrow."

"Can't you make any conquests at the table-d'hote?"

"Some of the men say pretty things to me, but as they all know how poor we are they are afraid to come to our room."

"And yet in spite of all you keep cheerful; you don't look sad like most of the unhappy. I congratulate you on your good spirits." Irene's tale was like the fair Stuard's story over again, and Marcoline, though she had taken rather too much champagne, was deeply moved at this picture of misery. She kissed the girl, telling her that I would not forsake her, and that in the meanwhile they would spend a pleasant night.

"Come! let us to bed!" said she; and after taking off her clothes she helped Irene to undress. I had no wish to fight, against two, and said that I wanted to rest. The fair Venetian burst out laughing and said,—

"Go to bed and leave us alone."

I did so, and amused myself by watching the two Bacchantes; but Irene, who had evidently never engaged in such a combat before, was not nearly so adroit as Marcoline.

Before long Marcoline brought Irene in her arms to my bedside, and told me to kiss her.

"Leave me alone, dearest," said I, "the punch has got into your head, and you don't know what you are doing."

This stung her; and urging Irene to follow her example, she took up a position in my bed by force; and as there was not enough room for three, Marcoline got on top of Irene, calling her her wife.

I was virtuous enough to remain a wholly passive spectator of the scene, which was always new to me, though I had seen it so often; but at last they flung themselves on me with such violence that I was obliged to give way, and for the most part of the night I performed my share of the work, till they saw that I was completely exhausted. We fell asleep, and I did not wake up till noon, and then I saw my two beauties still asleep, with their limbs interlaced like the branches of a tree. I thought with a sigh of the pleasures of such a sleep, and got out of bed gently for fear of rousing them. I ordered a good dinner to be prepared, and countermanded the horses which had been waiting several hours.

The landlord remembering what I had done for Madame Stuard guessed I was going to do the same for the Rinaldis, and left them in peace.

When I came back I found my two Lesbians awake, and they gave me such an amorous welcome that I felt inclined to complete the work of the night with a lover's good morning; but I began to feel the need of husbanding my forces, so I did nothing, and bore their sarcasms in silence till one o'clock, when I told them to get up, as we ought to have done at five o'clock, and here was two o'clock and breakfast not done.

"We have enjoyed ourselves," said Marcoline, "and time that is given to enjoyment is never lost."

When they were dressed, I had coffee brought in, and I gave Irene sixteen louis, four of which were to redeem her cloak. Her father and mother who had just dined came in to bid us good-day, and Irene proudly gave her father twelve louis telling him to scold her a little less in future. He laughed, wept, and went out, and then came back and said he found a good way of getting to Antibes at a small cost, but they would have to go directly, as the driver wanted to get to St. Andiol by nightfall.

"I am quite ready."

"No, dear Irene," said I, "you shall not go; you shall dine with your friend, and your driver can wait. Make him do so, Count Rinaldi; my niece will pay, will you not, Marcoline?"

"Certainly. I should like to dine here, and still better to put off our departure till the next day."

Her wishes were my orders. We had a delicious supper at five o'clock, and at eight we went to bed and spent the night in wantonness, but at five in the morning all were ready to start. Irene, who wore her handsome cloak, shed hot tears at parting from Marcoline, who also wept with all her heart. Old Rinaldi, who proved himself no prophet, told me that I should make a great fortune in England, and his daughter sighed to be in Marcoline's place. We shall hear of Rinaldi later on.

We drove on for fifteen posts without stopping, and passed the night at Valence. The food was bad, but Marcoline forgot her discomfort in talking of Irene.

"Do you know," said she, "that if it had been in my power I should have taken her from her parents. I believe she is your daughter, though she is not like you."

"How can she be my daughter when I have never known her mother?"

"She told me that certainly."

"Didn't she tell you anything else?"

"Yes, she told me that you lived with her for three days and bought her maidenhead for a thousand sequins."

"Quite so, but did she tell you that I paid the money to her father?"

"Yes, the little fool doesn't keep anything for herself. I don't think I should ever be jealous of your mistresses, if you let me sleep with them. Is not that a mark of a good disposition? Tell me."

"You have, no doubt, a good disposition, but you could be quite as good without your dominant passion."

"It is not a passion. I only have desires for those I love."

"Who gave you this taste?"

"Nature. I began at seven, and in the last ten years I have certainly had four hundred sweethearts."

"You begin early. But when did you begin to have male sweethearts?"

"At eleven."

"Tell me all about it."

"Father Molini, a monk, was my confessor, and he expressed a desire to know the girl who was then my sweetheart. It was in the carnival time, and he gave us a moral discourse, telling us that he would take us to the play if we would promise to abstain for a week. We promised to do so, and at the end of the week we went to tell him that we had kept our word faithfully. The next day Father Molini called on my sweetheart's aunt in a mask, and as she knew him, and as he was a monk and a confessor, we were allowed to go with him. Besides, we were mere children; my sweetheart was only a year older than I.

"After the play the father took us to an inn, and gave us some supper; and when the meal was over he spoke to us of our sin, and wanted to see our privates. 'It's a great sin between two girls,' said he, 'but between a man and a woman it is a venial matter. Do you know how men are made?' We both knew, but we said no with one consent. 'Then would you like to know?' said he. We said we should like to know very much, and he added, 'If you will promise to keep it a secret, I may be able to satisfy your curiosity.' We gave our promises, and the good father proceeded to gratify us with a sight of the riches which nature had lavished on him, and in the course of an hour he had turned us into women. I must confess that he understood so well how to work on our curiosity that the request came from us. Three years later, when I was fourteen, I became the mistress of a young jeweller. Then came your brother; but he got nothing from me, because he began by saying that he could not ask me to give him any favours till we were married."

"You must have been amused at that."

"Yes, it did make me laugh, because I did not know that a priest could get married; and he excited my curiosity by telling me that they managed it at Geneva. Curiosity and wantonness made me escape with him; you know the rest."

Thus did Marcoline amuse me during the evening, and then we went to bed and slept quietly till the morning. We started from Valence at five, and in the evening we were set down at the "Hotel du Parc" at Lyons.

As soon as I was settled in the pleasant apartments allotted to me I went to Madame d'Urfe, who was staying in the Place Bellecour, and said, as usual, that she was sure I was coming on that day. She wanted to know if she had performed the ceremonies correctly, and Paralis, of course, informed her that she had, whereat she was much flattered. The young Aranda was with her, and after I had kissed him affectionately I told the marchioness that I would be with her at ten o'clock the next morning, and so I left her.

I kept the appointment and we spent the whole of the day in close conference, asking of the oracle concerning her being brought to bed, how she was to make her will, and how she should contrive to escape poverty in her regenerated shape. The oracle told her that she must go to Paris for her lying-in, and leave all her possessions to her son, who would not be a bastard, as Paralis promised that as soon as I got to London an English gentleman should be sent over to marry her. Finally, the oracle ordered her to prepare to start in three days, and to take Aranda with her. I had to take the latter to London and return him to his mother, for his real position in life was no longer a mystery, the little rascal having confessed all; however, I had found a remedy for his indiscretion as for the treachery of the Corticelli and Possano.

I longed to return him to the keeping of his mother, who constantly wrote me impertinent letters. I also wished to take my daughter, who, according to her mother, had become a prodigy of grace and beauty.

After the oracular business had been settled, I returned to the "Hotel du Parc" to dine with Marcoline. It was very late, and as I could not take my sweetheart to the play I called on M. Bono to enquire whether he had sent my brother to Paris. He told me that he had gone the day before, and that my great enemy, Possano, was still in Lyons, and that I would do well to be on my guard as far as he was concerned.

"I have seen him," said Bono; "he looks pale and undone, and seems scarcely able to stand. 'I shall die before long,' said he, 'for that scoundrel Casanova has had me poisoned; but I will make him pay dearly for his crime, and in this very town of Lyons, where I know he will come, sooner or later.'

"In fact, in the course of half an hour, he made some terrible accusations against you, speaking as if he were in a fury. He wants all the world to know that you are the greatest villain unhung, that you are ruining Madame d'Urfe with your impious lies; that you are a sorcerer, a forger, an utter of false moneys, a poisoner—in short, the worst of men. He does not intend to publish a libellous pamphlet upon you, but to accuse you before the courts, alleging that he wants reparation for the wrongs you have done his person, his honour, and his life, for he says you are killing him by a slow poison. He adds that for every article he possesses the strongest proof.

"I will say nothing about the vague abuse he adds to these formal accusations, but I have felt it my duty to warn you of his treacherous designs that you may be able to defeat them. It's no good saying he is a miserable wretch, and that you despise him; you know how strong a thing calumny is."

"Where does the fellow live?"

"I don't know in the least."

"How can I find out?"

"I can't say, for if he is hiding himself on purpose it would be hard to get at him."

"Nevertheless, Lyons is not so vast a place."

"Lyons is a perfect maze, and there is no better hiding-place, especially to a man with money, and Possano has money."

"But what can he do to me?"

"He can institute proceedings against you in the criminal court, which would cause you immense anxiety and bring down your good name to the dust, even though you be the most innocent, the most just of men."

"It seems to me, then, that the best thing I can do will be to be first in the field."

"So I think, but even then you cannot avoid publicity."

"Tell me frankly if you feel disposed to bear witness to what the rascal has said in a court of justice."

"I will tell all I know with perfect truth."

"Be kind enough to tell me of a good advocate."

"I will give you the address of one of the best; but reflect before you do anything. The affair will make a noise."

"As I don't know where he lives, I have really no choice in the matter."

If I had known where he lived I could have had Possano expelled from
Lyons through the influence of Madame d'Urfe, whose relative, M. de la
Rochebaron, was the governor; but as it was, I had no other course than
the one I took.

Although Possano was a liar and an ungrateful, treacherous hound, yet I could not help being uneasy. I went to my hotel, and proceeded to ask for police protection against a man in hiding in Lyons, who had designs against my life and honour.

The next day M. Bono came to dissuade me from the course I had taken.

"For," said he, "the police will begin to search for him, and as soon as he hears of it he will take proceedings against you in the criminal courts, and then your positions will be changed. It seems to me that if you have no important business at Lyons you had better hasten your departure."

"Do you think I would do such a thing for a miserable fellow like Possano? No! I would despise myself if I did. I would die rather than hasten my departure on account of a rascal whom I loaded with kindnesses, despite his unworthiness! I would give a hundred louis to know where he is now."

"I am delighted to say that I do not know anything about it, for if I did I would tell you, and then God knows what would happen! You won't go any sooner; well, then, begin proceedings, and I will give my evidence by word of mouth or writing whenever you please."

I went to the advocate whom M. Bono had recommended to me, and told him my business. When he heard what I wanted he said,——

"I can do nothing for you, sir, as I have undertaken the case of your opponent. You need not be alarmed, however, at having spoken to me, for I assure you that I will make no use whatever of the information. Possano's plea or accusation will not be drawn up till the day after to-morrow, but I will not tell him to make haste for fear of your anticipating him, as I have only been informed of your intentions by hazard. However, you will find plenty of advocates at Lyons as honest as I am, and more skilled."

"Could you give me the name of one?"

"That would not be etiquette, but M. Bono, who seems to have kindly spoken of me with some esteem, will be able to serve you."

"Can you tell me where your client lives?"

"Since his chief aim is to remain hidden, and with good cause, you will see that I could not think of doing such a thing."

In bidding him farewell I put a louis on the table, and though I did it with the utmost delicacy he ran after me and made me take it back.

"For once in a way," I said to myself, "here's an honest advocate."

As I walked along I thought of putting a spy on Possano and finding out his abode, for I felt a strong desire to have him beaten to death; but where was I to find a spy in a town of which I knew nothing? M. Bono gave me the name of another advocate, and advised me to make haste.

"'Tis in criminal matters," said he, "and in such cases the first comer always has the advantage."

I asked him to find me a trusty fellow to track out the rascally Possano, but the worthy man would not hear of it. He shewed me that it would be dishonourable to set a spy on the actions of Possano's advocate. I knew it myself; but what man is there who has not yielded to the voice of vengeance, the most violent and least reasonable of all the passions.

I went to the second advocate, whom I found to be a man venerable not only in years but in wisdom. I told him all the circumstances of the affair, which he agreed to take up, saying he would present my plea in the course of the day.

"That's just what I want you to do," said I, "for his own advocate told me that his pleas would be presented the day after to-morrow."

"That, sir," said her "would not induce me to act with any greater promptness, as I could not consent to your abusing the confidence of my colleague."

"But there is nothing dishonourable in making use of information which one has acquired by chance."

"That may be a tenable position in some cases, but in the present instance the nature of the affair justifies prompt action. 'Prior in tempore, Potior in jure'. Prudence bids us attack our enemy. Be so kind, if you please, to call here at three o'clock in the afternoon."

"I will not fail to do so, and in the meanwhile here are six louis."

"I will keep account of my expenditure on your behalf."

"I want you not to spare money."

"Sir, I shall spend only what is absolutely necessary."

I almost believed that probity had chosen a home for herself amongst the
Lyons advocates, and here I may say, to the honour of the French bar, that I have never known a more honest body of men than the advocates of France.

At three o'clock, having seen that the plan was properly drawn up, I went to Madame d'Urfe's, and for four hours I worked the oracle in a manner that filled her with delight, and in spite of my vexation I could not help laughing at her insane fancies on the subject of her pregnancy. She was certain of it; she felt all the symptoms. Then she said how sorry she felt that she would not be alive to laugh at all the hypotheses of the Paris doctors as to her being delivered of a child, which would be thought very extraordinary in a woman of her age.

When I got back to the inn I found Marcoline very melancholy. She said she had been waiting for me to take her to the play, according to my promise, and that I should not have made her wait in vain.

"You are right, dearest, but an affair of importance has kept me with the marchioness. Don't be put out."

I had need of some such advice myself, for the legal affair worried me, and I slept very ill. Early the next morning I saw my counsel, who told me that my plea had been laid before the criminal lieutenant.

"For the present," said he, "there is nothing more to be done, for as we don't know where he is we can't cite him to appear."

"Could I not set the police on his track?"

"You might, but I don't advise you to do so. Let us consider what the result would be. The accuser finding himself accused would have to defend himself and prove the accusation he has made against you. But in the present state of things, if he does not put in an appearance we will get judgment against him for contempt of court and also for libel. Even his counsel will leave him in the lurch if he persistently refuses to shew himself."

This quieted my fears a little, and I spent the rest of the day with Madame d'Urfe, who was going to Paris on the morrow. I promised to be with her as soon as I had dealt with certain matters which concerned the honour of the Fraternity R. C..

Her great maxim was always to respect my secrets, and never to trouble me with her curiosity. Marcoline, who had been pining by herself all day, breathed again when I told her that henceforth I should be all for her.

In the morning M. Bono came to me and begged me to go with him to Possano's counsel, who wanted to speak to me. The advocate said that his client was a sort of madman who was ready to do anything, as he believed himself to be dying from the effects of a slow poison.

"He says that even if you are first in the field he will have you condemned to death. He says he doesn't care if he is sent to prison, as he is certain of coming out in triumph as he has the proof of all his accusations. He shews twenty-five louis which you gave him, all of which are clipped, and he exhibits documents dated from Genoa stating that you clipped a number of gold pieces, which were melted by M. Grimaldi in order that the police might not find them in your possession. He has even a letter from your brother, the abbe, deposing against you. He is a madman, a victim to syphilis, who wishes to send you to the other world before himself, if he can. Now my advice to you is to give him some money and get rid of him. He tells me that he is the father of a family, and that if M. Bono would give him a thousand louis he would sacrifice vengeance to necessity. He told me to speak to M. Bono about it; and now, sir what do you say?"

"That which my just indignation inspires me to say regarding a rascal whom I rescued from poverty, and who nevertheless pursues me with atrocious calumnies; he shall not have one single farthing of mine."

I then told the Genoa story, putting things in their true light, and adding that I could call M. Grimaldi as a witness if necessary.

"I have delayed presenting the plea," said the counsel, "to see if the scandal could be hushed up in any way, but I warn you that I shall now present it."

"Do so; I shall be greatly obliged to you."

I immediately called on my advocate, and told him of the rascal's proposal; and he said I was quite right to refuse to have any dealings with such a fellow. He added that as I had M. Bono as a witness I ought to make Possano's advocate present his plea, and I authorized him to take proceedings in my name.

A clerk was immediately sent to the criminal lieutenant, praying him to command the advocate to bring before him, in three days, the plea of one Anami, alias Pogomas, alias Possano, the said plea being against Jacques Casanova, commonly called the Chevalier de Seingalt. This document, to which I affixed my signature, was laid before the criminal lieutenant.

I did not care for the three days' delay, but my counsel told me it was always given, and that I must make up my mind to submit to all the vexation I should be obliged to undergo, even if we were wholly successful.

As Madame d'Urfe had taken her departure in conformity with the orders of Paralis, I dined with Marcoline at the inn, and tried to raise my spirits by all the means in my power. I took my mistress to the best milliners and dressmakers in the town, and bought her everything she took a fancy to; and then we went to the theatre, where she must have been pleased to see all eyes fixed on her. Madame Pernon, who was in the next box to ours, made me introduce Marcoline to her; and from the way they embraced each other when the play was over I saw they were likely to become intimate, the only obstacle to their friendship being that Madame Pernon did not know a word of Italian, and that Marcoline did not dare to speak a word of French for fear of making herself ridiculous. When we got back to the inn, Marcoline told me that her new friend had given her the Florentine kiss: this is the shibboleth of the sect.

The pretty nick-nacks I had given her had made her happy; her ardour was redoubled, and the night passed joyously.

I spent the next day in going from shop to shop, making fresh purchases for Marcoline, and we supped merrily at Madame Pernon's.

The day after, M. Bono came to see me at an early hour with a smile of content on his face.

"Let us go and breakfast at a coffee-house," said he; "we will have some discussion together."

When we were breakfasting he shewed me a letter written by Possano, in which the rascal said that he was ready to abandon proceedings provided that M. de Seingalt gave him a hundred louis, on receipt of which he promised to leave Lyons immediately.

"I should be a great fool," said I, "if I gave the knave more money to escape from the hands of justice. Let him go if he likes, I won't prevent him; but he had better not expect me to give him anything. He will have a writ out against him to-morrow. I should like to see him branded by the hangman. He has slandered me, his benefactor, too grievously; let him prove what he says, or be dishonoured before all men."

"His abandoning the proceedings," said M. Bono, "would in my opinion amount to the same thing as his failing to prove his charges, and you would do well to prefer it to a trial which would do your reputation no good, even if you were completely successful. And the hundred louis is nothing in comparison with the costs of such a trial."

"M. Bono, I value your advice very highly, and still more highly the kindly feelings which prompt you, but you must allow me to follow my own opinion in this case."

I went to my counsel and told him of the fresh proposal that Possano had made, and of my refusal to listen to it, begging him to take measures for the arrest of the villain who had vowed my death.

The same evening I had Madame Pernon and M. Bono, who was her lover, to sup with me; and as the latter had a good knowledge of Italian Marcoline was able to take part in the merriment of the company.

The next day Bono wrote to tell me that Possano had left Lyons never to return, and that he had signed a full and satisfactory retraction. I was not surprised to hear of his flight, but the other circumstance I could not understand. I therefore hastened to call on Bono, who showed me the document, which was certainly plain enough.

"Will that do?" said he.

"So well that I forgive him, but I wonder he did not insist on the hundred louis."

"My dear sir, I gave him the money with pleasure, to prevent a scandalous affair which would have done us all harm in becoming public. If I had told you nothing, you couldn't have taken any steps in the matter, and I felt myself obliged to repair the mischief I had done in this way. You would have known nothing about it, if you had said that you were not satisfied. I am only too glad to have been enabled to skew my friendship by this trifling service. We will say no more about it."

"Very good," said I, embracing him, "we will say no more, but please to receive the assurance of my gratitude."

I confess I felt much relieved at being freed from this troublesome business.

The End